==============================
Cover Photo by: Sasha Davidson, Creative Director
Tiverton House - www.JamaicaEscapes.com
==============================

More
Jamaica Old-Time
Sayings

by:
Edna Bennett

More Jamaica Old-Time Sayings

Edna Bennett

Edited by Ken Jones, O.D., and J.P.

TRAFFORD PUBLISHING
166 Liberty Drive
Bloomington
Indiana 47403

Order this book online at www.trafford.com
or email orders@trafford.com

Most Trafford titles are also available at major online book retailers.

Printed in the United States of America.

ISBN: 978-1-4269-4546-5 (sc)
ISBN: 978-1-4269-4545-8 (hc)
ISBN: 978-1-4269-4547-2 (e)

Library of Congress Control Number: 2010914949

*Our mission is to efficiently provide the world's finest, most comprehensive book publishing
service, enabling every author to experience success. To find out how to publish your
book, your way, and have it available worldwide, visit us online at www.trafford.com*

Trafford rev. 10/06/2010

 www.trafford.com

North America & international
toll-free: 1 888 232 4444 (USA & Canada)
phone: 250 383 6864 ♦ fax: 812 355 4082

Contents

HISTORICAL PERSPECTIVE OF JAMAICA WITH A SYNOPIC VIEW OF THE PATOIS OR "OTHER" JAMAICAN LANGUAGE

Winsome Morgan-Bartley, Ph. D

Christopher Columbus, a name synonymous with the birth of the New World, landed on this island in 1494. August 10, 1494, like any other day, found the island's Indians routinely occupied in their daily chores. Startled they were by these strange and unknown beings, which remained a torment in their lives for many unbearable years.

Yes, these Indians became forcibly subjugated to the Spaniard's harsh change of culture and before long succumbed to suicide, genocide or merely found comfort in the mountainous terrain. The Spanish rule lasted up to the middle of the 17th century, when in 1655 the English interrupted a tightly supervised political system.

With the coming of the English, the Jamaican society was temporarily dismantled, giving way to a preferred English System, having a strong collaboration of a rigid political and economic base. Embedded in the day to day running of the economy was the urgency to become wealthy and powerful; hence with the extinction of most of the Indians and a brief exploitation of the White indentured servants, the African peoples were introduced as laborers under the grueling and inhumane slavery system.

The fabric of this slave society was what determined the outcome of the Jamaican culture today. Here one found a society that was rigidly divided according to the coulor of one's skin, an unfortunate distinction between the whites, the colored and the blacks. This clear-cut division was not only evident in religion, distribution of wealth and politics, to name a few, but also in language and education.

Education was denied from the blacks; hence the lack of communication between them at the accepted English language level. Subsequently, the birth of the Jamaican Patois became evident. The Patois is a derivative of the English language and the West African languages. Here the slaves conveniently merged these two languages as a means of communication among their black counterparts and their white slavemasters. If there is nothing else that has impacted on the Jamaican society, the Patois has, and is often referred to as the 'other' language, spoken by nearly 100% of the Jamaican population.

The Patois marginalized you, if you did not speak properly (meaning the English language), it was likely to be held against you, if you did not speak the Queen's English; hence you were seen as an outcast of the society. The Patois however, though held dormant, has not been inactive or dead. It is a very expressive and colorful language daunted with multiple figurative speeches, and is spoken in every 'nook and cranny' of the society (i.e. a wide cross section of the society)

So the Africans came and undoubtedly influenced the country's culture. Yes, slavery was abolished in the early 19th century, but because of the need for laborers to continue planting sugar cane, the East Indians, the Chinese, and Europeans were recruited, thereby adding to what became known as a multi-racial society – (a mixture of many races). This explains why our motto is "Out of many, one people".

In 1962 Jamaica oozed its way into independence from British colonialism and today enjoys a political stability with two dominant parties – The Jamaican Labor Party, and The People's' National Party.

Presently, the leader of the Government (The Prime Minister) is the Right Honorable Bruce Golding of the Jamaica Labor Party.

DEDICATION

To the memory of my parents and to my family, without whose
love and support my life would have been incomplete

FOREWORD

Mek Yu Ears Eat Grass!

This book is compiled and written in response to that deep longing which from time to time is felt by all sojourners - in this case, Jamaicans.

Far from their native surroundings - the hills and valleys of home, the peaceful countryside, the noisy towns, friends and relatives who share their joys and pain - Jamaicans, like other people, experience that tugging at the heart that can only be assuaged by pleasant memories.

As an island people, most of us have grown up close to each other, with ample opportunity for the rich to learn the ways of the poor, for the educated to understand the manners of the unlettered, for the city dweller to appreciate the informality of his country cousin, and for all of us to live together as one.

True, we do not always live out the true meaning of unity. Often, we are divided by the struggle that arises when there are "more dogs than bones." Although sometimes we demonstrate the traits of "crabs in a barrel," clawing at each other in the bid to rise to the top, this is not our true nature.

Most of us were raised in humble circumstances; and we never knew the urge of bitter rivalry until faced with the stern demands of adulthood. Many of us, perforce, were cut too soon from school or from our mother's apron strings and that made the challenge of life harder. But it also gave us character and a sturdiness, which in most cases has earned us varying degrees of success.

We owe much of that success to the slower pace at which we moved in childhood days. Then we had time to play and to exchange ideas on the long walk back from school, or swap tales that had been handed down to us. We improvised, made use of what we had, enjoyed our heritage and we were not dazzled by the glitter of larger, richer, distant lands. Our world was quiet. Our ears could "eat grass," and we did not have to strain them to catch the wisdom of our elders.

That has changed. A generation comes into the electronic age, endowed with a wider vista and a narrower vision. Growth is fast and age comes quickly. Often transplanted before their roots have quite matured, the young are frequently without the cultural anchor so necessary in time of storm.No need to wonder at the confusion. As it is better to ponder than to wonder, I have joined my friends in pondering; and we are agreed that a people without knowledge and appreciation for their culture is like a tree without roots, unable to withstand the winds of change.

We wish to keep the culture alive, to remind those who have forgotten and to help instruct those who never knew. We are not unique in this endeavor. There are many who have striven or still strive toward this end; and we, having benefited from their example, feel obliged to continue the work.

In the name of all those who consciously try to keep our culture alive, I urge you to take five, cock up yu foot, and mek yu ears eat grass, and 'member what yu old people used to say.

Ken Jones, C.D., J.P

ACKNOWLEDGMENTS

My deepest gratitude is due to the many persons whose encouragement, contributions and interest have made it possible for me to produce this book. Special thanks to the editor, Ken Jones.

His experience and enthusiasm helped to upgrade and transform my hobby horse into a vehicle for deeper study. His work on the glossary is particularly helpful and will no doubt provide amusement and enlightenment for many.

Raphael Douglas, who, like Ken Jones, is a life-long friend of mine, labored behind the scenes and was a constant source of support. I am fascinated by the fact that we grew up together, got our primary education at the same school, went our separate ways for many years, but met again, by chance, to collaborate in this effort.

INTRODUCTION

Like a Kitchen without a Knife...

Growing up in my native Jamaica, I had parents whom I enjoy describing as "Victorian." They were part of the matriarchal society and for both of them; discipline was the order of the day.

Father's role seemed a lot easier than that of my mother, the matriarch. He was the breadwinner upon whom everyone waited. He was expected to discipline the children, but only when this could not be done by mother. He was loved by all, but as the court of last resort, his discipline sometimes meant corporate punishment.

Mother had full responsibility for the discipline of the brood, four boys and five girls - and she had to find the tools to do the job. This book is about one of the tools frequently used in bringing up our family; the good old Jamaican proverbs.

Some of what you read has religious origins. Some are adapted; others point to the law of cause-and-effect, and most are pure logic. Regardless of the source, one thing is sure; each one carries a powerful message.

This condensation of collective wisdom is presented in Jamaican dialect with English translations. Most are used island wide. Others are subject to variations, depending upon which part of the country they may be from. By no means a total collection, it will spur the memory and take readers back to the roots of their culture.

To better appreciate this book, one should look at the Jamaican language and the way it developed out of a mixture of African and English words. The African slaves, coming from different tribes, had to find a common tongue with which to communicate among themselves and with the slave master and their overseers. The new Jamaicans developed their own system; it was called Patois.

Jamaican dialect, influenced by three hundred years of British rule, has a strong West African base, particularly Twi and Ashanti.

The proverbs, more often than not, are related to animals, birds and insects. They are very homey - domestic if you will - and always to the point. A Jamaican home without them would indeed be like a kitchen without a knife.

A

Advice is of no use to a fool.
A fool is incapable a heeding advice

A fas' mek Anansi live a house top.
According to an Anansi story, Anansi interfered with Brer Tiger's business, was chased and took refuge in the ceiling.

A hint to a ole mule is as good as a lick.
A man with experience does not need too much teaching.

After de rain come de sunshine.
A consolation to the unhappy that happiness will come after the sorrow has passed.

After mi nable string no cut pon it.
A response to indicate that the solicited item is one without which the solicitor can live.
Version: *After doctor nevva put mi pon it.*

A hungry man is a' angry man.
A person badly in need of something usually gets impatient with those who stand in his way.

Alligator lay egg but 'im a no fowl.
One should not judge a person solely on the basis of one act.

All kind of fish nyam man, but only shark get de blame.
A person often gets blamed only because of his reputation for doing wrong.

A nuh because cow no have tongue mek 'im nuh talk.
Silence is sometimes dictated by prudence rather than by ignorance.

A nuh same day leaf drop inna water dat it rotten.
It may take a long time before an injured party gets revenge.

A nuh one time monkey want wife.
Always show gratitude or risk being ignored the next time assistance is needed.
Version: *A no one day dawg have heart b'un.*

Ants follow fat.
It is normal for people to pursue things they like.

Anybody ever see mi dyin' trial?
Are you taking note of my calamity?

Any cry wil' do fi burial.
Any weeping is acceptable at a funeral, meaning that in a crisis one may use whatever resources are available.

Any drum knock under water bottom, de soun' mus' come a top.
A man's feelings, however well -hidden, will one day come to light.

Any side o' the bed dat yu sleep 'pon las' night, sleep 'pon de same side tonight.
You have just missed a disaster. You must have slept on the lucky side of the bed last night.

Anyt'ing yu hear nayga say, if a no so it go, is near so it go.
There is a bit of truth to any rumor that is widely circulated.

Anywhe' it mawga it bruk.
The weakest link is where the chain will break.

Anywhere water walk one time, it wi' walk again.
History never fails to repeat itself

A promise is a comfort to a fool.
A fool cannot distinguish between a promise and an attempt to hoodwink him.

As a man thinketh so is he.
A person's demeanor reflects how that person feels about himself.

A so yu live, a so yu die.
The manner of a person's death is often related to the ways of his living. For instance, if one lives peacefully, chances are that one will die peacefully.

Ashes cold, dawg mek 'im bed inna it.
When a fire is out and the ashes no longer hot, it can be handled without caution. Therefore one need not be afraid of a strong man grown feeble or a danger that has passed.

Ask me no question, I tell you no lie.
If you don't ask a question, you cannot get a misleading answer.

A swif' why wass-wass nuh mek honey.
According to folklore, the bee taught the wasp to make a honeycomb, but the wasp flew off before learning how to make honey.

A wise head keep a still tongue.
A wise person knows when to remain silent, and does not tell everything he knows.

B

Back a dawg a dawg, before dawg a Mister Dawg.
Some disrespect a powerful man behind his back but bow in his presence.

Back no know de goodness of old shut till it tear off.
One seldom sees the value of an old item until it is lost or becomes unserviceable.

3

Bad luck worse dan obeah.
> One beset by bad luck is worse off than one subject to witchcraft.

Bad wud an' ears hole don't 'gree.
> Curse words are likely to stir up anger.

Ban' yu belly.
> Be prepared for hardships.

Barking dog 'ave nuh time fi bite.
> Those who spend too much time in squabbles, have very little time for personal achievements.

Before good food waste, mek belly bus'.
> Excuse for gluttony. Said to have been stated by Anansi at a feast for Brer Tiger.

Before pra-pra mek quarrel, mek grung sipple.
> Akin to the throwing of oil on troubled water.

Before yu fall dung, ketch macca.
> Choose the lesser of two evils.

Before yu marry keep two eye' open; afterwards shut one.
> Check out all the faults of your partner before marriage. After that, it is better to overlook them.

Beggar from beggar can' get rich.
> One cannot improve one's position by depending on an equally poor person.

Beg water can' bwile cow skin.
> Begging is a short-term answer to problems and should not be used as a long-term solution.

Belief kill an' belief cure.
> Faith can work wonders.

Belly full mek potato hav' skin.
A satisfied person becomes very choosy.

Ben' de tree when it young.
Start training your child early.

Better dem laugh after yu when yu right, dan cry over yu when yu wrong.
Advice against being too mindful of criticism.

Better fi fowl say dawg dead than dawg say fowl dead.
The fowl cannot be blamed for the dog's death, but the same is not true of the dog.

Better fi have lion-heart than pig head.
Better to be strong than to be stubborn.

Better late dan never.
Better to get late action than to have no action at all.

Better short pence than short a sense.
Better to be poor than foolish.

Better yu ded lef it dan live fi want it.
It is always good to have enough to spare.

Between de devil an' de deep blue sea.
Version: Caught between a rock and a hard place.

Big blanket mek man sleep late.
Luxury encourages laziness.

Birds of a fedda flock togedda.
People sharing similar values are attracted to each other.

Blackbud lef 'im ticks and pick fi cow own.
Used in reference to one who helps others before helping himself.

Black fowl can lay white egg.
The unexpected can take place.

Black fowl no fi yu, yu call 'im John Crow.
Reference to one who finds fault with something he cannot have.
Version: *Sour grapes.*

Blood t'icker dan water.
There is generally more concern for a blood relative than for a stranger.

Box shit outta hog mout'.
Having to do this is a clear sign of poverty and desperation.

Bud can' fly pon one wing.
This excuse is usually used to justify a second drink.

Bud fly too fas', 'im pass 'im nes'.
This is another way of saying 'aste makes waste'.

Bull foot bruk 'im nyam wid monkey.
One in trouble is forced to humble himself.

Bull get ole, 'im feed a fence side.
When one is old and disabled, he has to be content with whatever may be available.

Bull horn nevva too heavy fi bull head.
One should never be tired of doing his own work.

Butcher cow nevva say 'im very well.
Faced with being slaughtered, the cow will claim to be sick.

Buy beef yu buy bone; buy lan' you buy rockstone.
In life the good is often accompanied by the bad.

C

Callalu swear fi ole 'oman, ole 'oman swear fi callalu.
Reference to those who threaten to fight, however helpless they may seem,

Carry go, bring come bring mysery.
A reference to the act of taking tales to and from different persons.

Cashew can' bear guava.
What you sow is what you should expect to reap.

Cas' yu bread on de waters and you will fine it many days after.
If you give you will receive, even if it takes a long time.

Chair fall dung, bench git up.
The decline of the mighty may be an opportunity for the humble to rise.

Chicken merry, hawk de near.
In celebrating success, one should be prepared for sudden dangers.
Version: *In the midst of life, we are in death.*
Chim cherry bear cedar.
Some children bear no resemblance of their parents

Chips never fly far from de block.
A child is likely to exhibit the characteristics of its elders.
Version: *Blood follow vein.*

Circumstances alter cases.
Different situations require different handlings.

Clean pants an' dutty draws.
Commonly used in reference to a hypocrite.

Cockeye man a king inna blin' man country.
A leader's performance must be superior to the performance of his followers.

Cock hav' spur but 'im can' ride jackass.
Good tools do not necessarily make a good workman.

Cock mek more noise dan fowl wha' lay de egg.
Some people like to take credit for the accomplishments of others.

Cock mout' kill cock.
Talking too much can land a person in trouble. The cock was killed because of crowing and drawing attention to himself.

Cockroach inna trouble, 'im hide a fowl-house.
Desperation can lead one to ask an enemy for help.

Cockroach never right in front o' fowl.
It is useless to plead innocence before a prejudiced judge.

Cockroach no business inna fowl back yard.
A person should not become involved in a situation controlled by his enemies.

Cockroach keep dance but 'im no ask fowl.
One should never put oneself in a position to be hurt by one's enemies.

Commander coco and white yam nuh bear togedda.
If two good eaters share the same plate, neither will get enough.

Coming events cas' shadows.
In life there are no real secrets.

Coming to come.
Nearing the target. A reference to someone or something improving.

Consequential mek crab no have head.
Crab asked the gods for a head and, getting it, exhibited such pride that the gift was withdrawn in disgust.

Cotton tree ever so big, yet lilly ax cut 'im dung.
One is never too big to be tripped up by a smaller person.

Cotton tree fall dung, nanny goat jump over it.
When the mighty falls, the humblest may take advantage of him.

Cotton tree no know how 'im bottom stan, so 'Im no call no breeze.
One should not undertake a task without first checking on his ability to handle it.

Cousin and cousin bwile good soup.
A match between second cousins is said to be good, although first cousins should not marry.

Cow get ol', dem tie 'im wid wiss.
When a cow is feeble, it is easy to restrain him. Similarly, one who has lost his vigor and mental capacity is easily manipulated. In some places the proverb substitutes "plantain bark" for wiss.

Cow give bucket a milk den kick it over.
This alludes to someone who does good, then cancels the benefit with a counteraction.

Cow nuh know de use o 'im tail 'til 'im lose it.
A cow without a tail cannot defend himself against insects.

Cow read 'im law inna 'im belly.
Not every plan should be made public.

Coward man keep soun' bone.
One who does not get into a fight cannot be injured by it.

Crab no walk 'im can' get fat; walk too much 'im lose 'im claw.
One cannot win without taking chances. However, persistence in this increases the chances of losing.

Crab walk too much, 'im go a cutacoo.
A restless person soon gets into trouble.

Crow see mawga cow, 'im go roas' plaintain fi 'im.
One who appears to be dying will often attract someone waiting to inherit his legacy.

Cup nuh bruk, cawfee nuh dash wey.
When a cup is broken, the contents are lost. If a cup is not broken and the coffee is not lost, then no damage is done.

Cuss-cuss can' bore hole inna man skin.
Curses won't cause physical injury to anyone.

Cutacoo full, 'oman laugh.
In times of plenty, a woman is pleased with her man.

Cut eye, cut eye can' cut mi in two.
An evil look from anyone will not cause physical injury.

Cut yu coatee 'cording to yu cloth.
A tailor cannot make a suit bigger than the material will allow. Hence, one's business must be conducted in keeping with one's resources.

D

Dawg drink water fi yu; but Massa God a fi all a we.
A dog drinks for himself; God is for everyone. Meaning, each person must look after his own interest.

Dawg 'mong doctor, cockroach 'mong shaver.
Stick to the company in which you are most comfortable.

Dawg 'ave money, 'im tek it buy cheese.
One unaccustomed to having money tends to spend it foolishly.

Dawg 'ave shine teet', 'im laugh afta butcha.
Shining teeth shows that a dog is well-fed and can afford to be independent of the butcher.

Dawg 'ave too much owner, 'im go a bed widout suppa.
When everyone has responsibility for a task, it is often done by no one.

Dawg mawga but 'im head big.
This is used to describe a poor but pompous person.

Dawg nevver nyam dawg.
Members of a family do not normally act against each other.

Dawg nyam yu suppa.
An expression to indicate that one is in a lot of trouble.

Dawg say betta dan buy nankeen fi sixpence, gi doubloon fi bone.
Spend your money on what is useful to you.

Dawg see firestick, 'im skin 'im teet'.
The firestick is used to see whether the dog is real or is a ghost.

Dawg sweat but 'im long hair cover it.
One may be calm on the outside yet quite angry on the inside.

Dawg walk too much, 'im lose 'im share.
One who does not stick to a task cannot get good results.

Dawg wey bring a bone, wi' carry a bone.
Never be too trusting with one who brings news as he is likely to carry news as well.

Dawg wid bruk foot will find 'im massa yard.
In times of trouble, one tends to seek comfort and assistance from those closest to him.

De bes' passion is compassion.
This lauds the virtue of compassion.

De bigga de fish, de more oil it tek fi fry.
It takes more strength and cunning to trap a powerful enemy.

De blessin' of a man is wey 'im give 'wey.
Our blessings are measured according to our generosity.

De cheapes' always come to be the deares'.
In trying to save on cost, one tends to sacrifice quality.

De chips nevva fly far from de block.
Most children exhibit some traits of one or another parent.

De cost tek 'way de taste.
When one has to pay too much for anything, one does not enjoy it as much as when one is satisfied with the price.

De devil always fin' work fi idle hands.
The temptation to get into trouble is strongest amongst those who have very little to do.

De devil an' 'im wife a fight fi mackerel bone.
Used to describe uncertain weather conditions in which sunshine and rain clouds appear with thunder.

De difference between a flute and a fiddle is the sound.
The difference between one person and another is in the essence of one's being.

De eye of de master fatten de calf.
One's business is best looked after by oneself.

De falling of one is de rising of another.
Whenever someone loses, someone else gains

De foot o' the owner manure de field.
Equivalent to "the eye of the master fattens the calf."

De higher monkey climb, the more 'im expose 'imself.
The more a person gets into public notice, the more carefully will others observe his shortfalls.

De longest liver will see de most.
As one grows older, the more experience he/she will have.

De miller's hogs are fat, but we don't know whose corn fattened them.
This is an advice not to be jealous of one's success.

De mills of God grind slowly.
God's justice is usually slow in coming.

De more yu chop breadfruit root, de more 'im spring.
Used in reference to a resilient person who is like the breadfruit tree that tends to spring a new plant whenever the tree is cut.

De more yu live the more yu learn.
Wisdom comes with age.

De more yu look, de less yu se'.
Concentrating on one thing allows other things to pass unnoticed.

De nearer to church, de farder from God.
Some church-goers use religion to cover a multitude of sins.

De rat that eat the least live the longest.
A greedy person will die early.

De same knife stick sheep, stick goat.
One should never consider oneself immune as long as bad company is around.

De same sugar weh sweeten tongue, rotten teeth.
Most things that bring joy are capable of bringing sorrow in equal measure.

De want is more than de worth.
Because of a great need, a man will pay more for an article than its worth.

De woun' wi' heal, but it leave scar.
One will eventually overcome, but never forget a bad experience.

Dead hog nuh fraid o' hot water.
When a hog is dead, it makes no difference how his carcass is treated. So it is with some people who are not moved by criticism.

Dead man tell no tale.
A dead man cannot be called upon to give evidence for or against anyone.

Deaf ears gi' liad trouble.
A liar must speak loudly for the deaf to hear. However, in doing so, he broadcasts his story so that others may bear witness.

Dem eye mek four.
They met face to face.

Dem short o' singer when dem put peacock inna choir.
This means that the situation is a desperate one, because the peacock's voice is not a musical one.

Dis can' pay red herring taxes.
This is not a productive exercise.

Donkey say de worl' no level.
Donkeys are always selected to carry heavy loads over rough terrain and are therefore aware that not everyone is accorded equal treatment in life.

Don' bite off more than you can chew.
In whatever you do, always be moderate in your approach.

Don' cut off yu nose fi spite you face.
Do not hurt yourself in an effort to get revenge.

Don' draw chokie mek bud see yu.
Do not set a trap while the prey is looking on.

Don' draw mi tongue!
Do not provoke me into making a retort.

Don' drink yu soup when it' hot.
Do not make hasty decisions.

Don' hang yu hat wey yu can' reach it.
Don't incur debts that are difficult to repay.

Don' jump down mi throat!
This is a rebuke to one interrupting the speech of another.

Don' know "a" from bull-foot.
This is often used to describe an illiterate person.

Don' post me!
Don't keep me waiting!

Drum done play, Jackie done dance.
Performance tends to decline when incentives are removed.

Drunken man talk de truth.
Someone in a state of drunkenness tends not to care about the consequences of truth.

Dry drink better dan sermon.

Used by someone who resents being preached at because of his short-comings.

Duck an' fowl feed togedda, but dem no roost togedda.
Friendship is not always intimate.

Duppy know who fi frighten.
People tend to attack those whom they believe cannot retaliate.

Dutty nah kill yu unless it drop pon yu.
Dirt on the skin is not as dangerous as dirt falling on the head.

E

Easy come, easy go.
Things lightly got are lightly lost.

Easy squeeze mek no riot.
A gentle approach averts confrontation.
Version: *A soft answer turns away wrath.*

Empty barrel mek de mos' noise.
A barrel will make a louder sound when empty than when full. Similarly, a noisy person is said to have less in his head.

Empty bag can' stan' up; full bag can' ben'.
A bag will sag or collapse unless it is filled with something. The first part of the phrase is usually quoted to indicate that a hungry person cannot perform efficiently. Alternately, one who has eaten too much is in the same predicament.

Empty pot can' bwile over.
The poor never have enough to give away.

Every dawg a lion inna 'im maasa yard.
Even a scrawny mutt will bark loudly and bare his teeth once he is within the confines of his home. A man's home is his castle.
Version: Cock crow loudes' pon 'im own dung hill.

Every dawg 'ave 'im day, an' every puss 'im four o'clock.
There will come a day for each of us to rejoice, regardless of our status.

Every day bucket go a well, one day de bottom mus' drop out.
All activities have a lifespan. In some parts of Jamaica, water for domestic use is obtained from stand-pipes located in the village square or from wells, springs, rivers, or from rooftops during rainfall. In each case, a bucket is the container most often used to "catch the water." Green leaves are put on top to minimize splashing.

Every day devil help t'ief, one day God help watchman.
A man cannot always get away with his misdemeanors.

Every day no Christmas an' every day no rainy day.
Every day cannot be enjoyable, nor is every day a period of tough times.

Every heart know 'im own sorrow.
The best account of suffering comes from the sufferer.

Every hoe got 'im stick a bush.
There is an ideal partner for everyone.
Version: Every donkey 'ave 'im sankey; every 'stinkin' fish 'ave dem buyer.

Every John-Crow t'ink 'im pickney white.
Every parent thinks his child is better than his neighbor's offspring.

Every man fah 'imself God fah all of us,
Man is selfish. God is not.

Every man to 'is own order.
Every person has his own agenda, made up to his own liking.

Every mickle mek a muckle.
Every little bit counts and should not be ignored.

Every sore foot 'ave 'im blue stone.
There is a cure for every ailment.

Everyt'ing happen fi a wise purpose.
There is a good reason for every occurrence, however bad it may seem.

Every t'ief hones' 'til dem ketch 'im.
A thief can claim innocence until the day he is caught.

Every tub stan' up pon 'im own bottom.
Each person should exercise some degree of self-reliance.

Everywhere yu turn, macca juk yu.
Reference to a man who finds trouble on every side, no matter how he tries to escape.

Eye can' tek meat out a kreng-kreng.
Simply looking at an object will not hurt it.

F

Fall off a high table.
Used when ones social status falls below the status of his ancestors.

Far pass mek okra spwile.
It is not good to be too far from the place of business.

Feas' today, famine tomorrow.
It is unwise to spend all of your resources without thought of the needs of the next day.

Finga neva sa', "Look ya!" it always say "Look deh!"

The accusing finger is always pointed at others, never at oneself. A note of caution is added by the reminder that while one finger points outward, the others point inward.

Version: Lickle finga say, "Look deh!" big t'umb say, "Look ya!"

Finga stink, you can' cut it off.

One cannot disown close relatives even when their performance falls short of expectations.

Fire a muss-muss tail, 'im seh a cool breeze.

Muss-muss is a Jamaican word for mouse. This saying refers to one's misinterpretation of events - failing to see danger because of apparent success.

Fisherman nevva say 'im fish stink.

One is inclined to defend his reputation, however bad it may be.

Follow fashion mek monkey lose 'im tail.

This warns of the danger of imitating actions with which one is unfamiliar.

Version: Follow fashion Juba never bwile good soup.

Juba is the name for women born on Monday.

Follow wass-wass, yu bun down yu house.

Used in reference to the practice of destroying wasp nests with fire at the end of a pole. One should be careful in dealing with enemies.

Fool nuh 'ave use fi advice.

A fool thinks that he has all the answers and therefore will not accept advice.

Foolish man drink soup wid fork, eat rice wid pin, eat parch corn, an' lick 'im finga.

It is considered foolish to give oneself unnecessary work.

Fools have feasts. Wise men eat.
Fools are always at the mercy of the wise.

Forgettin' is one ting, forgiving is another ting.
It is easier to forgive than to forget.

Fowl never see egg, 'im call white stone egg.
An inexperienced person is likely to make silly errors.

Fowl done nyam, 'im wipe 'im mout' a grung.
This shows ingratitude and bad manners.
Some give the direct opposite meaning to the proverb.

Fowl never mash 'im pickney hot.
A hen never hurts her chicken even when she steps on it. So a mother who will scold will not intentionally hurt her offspring.

Fowl scratch too much, 'im find 'im gran'ma skeleton.
Being too inquisitive can lead to the finding of unpleasant things.

From saltfish was a shingle house.
This refers to a very very long time ago.
Versions: From de devil was a bwoy: From mi eye de a mi knee.

Full belly tell hungry belly, "Tek heart."
It is easy for one to suggest patience when one's problems are solved.

Furda distance, betta aquaintance.
In some instances, a casual relationship is better than a close one.

Fus laugh a no laugh, las' laugh a laugh.
The man who laughs at the end of the action is better than one who laughed at the beginning.

Fus wud go a law.
Judgement is based on the first statement rather than later amendments.

G

Give yu a inch, yu tek a ell.
An ell is an old English measure of about forty-five inches. The proverb applies to one who abuses privilege by exceeding what is reasonable.

Goat feed 'way 'im tie.
One is obliged to make do with what is within one's reach.

Goat say 'im woulda laugh, but everybody woulda know say 'im no have top teet'.
The ignorant is advised to remain silent and not reveal his shortcomings.

God bigger dan any problem.
God can see you through any problem, regardless of its size.

God a'mighty no love ugly.
The Lord will not be in favor of ugly behavior.

God look afta babies an' fools.
Babies and fools have Divine protection at all times.

God naw sleep.
A reminder that the Almighty sees every act of every one, and that he will judge accordingly

God neva shut a door an' no open a window.
With God as our source, all is not lost

Good company keep late 'ours.
Time passes quickly when good friends are enjoying themselves.

Good frien' better dan pocket-money.
A loyal friend is to be valued more than money.

Greedy choke puppy.
Used when one who fails because of taking on more than one
can manage.

Green bush can' bwile pot.
Green bush will not produce a flame, nor will an immature
person perform as well as one with experience.

Grey hog a de hardes' hog fi dead.
This animal is said to embody spirits used for obeah and is
therefore more cunning than others.

Grudgeful mek patoo lay egg.
Envy can lead a person to put a strain on himself.

Guilty concience nuh need no accuser.
He who commits a misdemeanor needs no accuser, because his
conscience will lead him to show his guilt.

H

Hair of de same dawg.
This is supposed to be good for a dog bite. It also justifies a drink
of the same liquor responsible for one's hangover.

Habi, habi no wanti, and wanti wanti no habi.
Sometimes those who have something do not want it, while
others who want it can't have it.

Half-a-foot man dance near 'im fambly.
One who is unsure of himself tends to keep near to his family
or friends.

Hand go, packy come.
Give a little get a lot. Go with empty hand, come back with packy.
Packy is a small fruit akin to the calabash.

Happiness begin at 'ome
Begin your search for happiness in your own home.

Hard-ears pickney go a market two time.
A child who does not listen to instructions will have to run his errand twice if he makes a mistake.

Hasty fi rich you fall in a ditch.
Shooting for a target too soon can spoil the whole project.
Version: *Haste mek waste.*

He who feels it knows it.
One who has lived through an experience has first hand knowledge of that experience.

Hen hatch duck egg, but 'im can't teach duck pickney fi swim.
There is a limit to everyone's capabilities.

Her tongue is like a Panya (Spanish) machete.
Usually used in reference to a woman who switches from side to side during a dispute, but is also used to describe a man of similar disposition.
Note: The Spanish machette is one that has been sharpened on both sides.

High seat kill Miss Barnes puss.
A warning not to over-project one's self.

Him can' mash ants
Used in reference to a quiet, cautious person.

Him coco roas' an' butter.
He has no problem.

Him no lif' straw.
He is an idler.

Hog no have water fi wah 'imself, but have it fi gi wey.
Criticism of one who has very little, but is offering to help.

Hog run for 'im life, dawg run fi 'im character.
Different circumstances can produce the same results.

Hog wash inna de firs' water 'im fin'.
A pig will wallow in the first water he finds, however muddy it may be. Likewise, a man in need will grab the first opportunity he gets.

Hope wi no more strangers.
Used to express a wish for a closer relationship with a new acquaintance.

Horse a gallop, no hear wey 'im back foot a say.
A perslon in the lead should take time to know about those who are behind. Otherwise, he might find himself out of touch.

Horse dead, cow fat.
When the horse dies, there is more for the cow to eat.
Version: The falling of one is the rising of another.

Horse never too good fi carry 'im own grass.
One should never be ashamed to perform a menial task for oneself.

Hot needle bun t'read.
Version: Haste makes waste.

Howdy and tenky bruk no square.
Being polite, saying "how-do-you-do" and "thank you", never hurts.

Humble calves suck de mos' milk.
Version: Patient man ride jackass.

Hungry belly mek monkey blow fire.
Hard times lead one to improvise.
Version: *Necessity is the mother of invention.*

Hungry dawg eat roas' corn.
Dire circumstances will force a person to do the unusual.
Version: *Hungry belly mek monkey blow fire.*

Hurry hurry bud nevva buil' good nes'.
This is the advice usually given to newlyweds, regarding home making.

I

I nevva drink me soup when it hot.
I like to carry out my tasks in a timely fashion.

If a egg, mi inna de red.
The use of this phrase is expresssing a desire to be in the center of things, regardless.

If breeze no blow, yu no see fowl back.
A person's true character is revealed in times of stress.
Version: Rain a fall, breeze a blow, chicken batty out a door.

If donkey bray after yu, no bray after 'im.
Two wrongs do not make a right.

If fish come from river bottom an' tell you alligator have fever, believe 'im.
Better to act on the advice of one with true experience than to risk the danger of finding out for yourself.

If 'im stomach no sick, wha' yu a vomit fah?
If a person is not worried by his own problem, there is no need for another to be concerned.

If John Crow never know 'im coulda pass out abbey seed, 'im wouda never swallow it.
A man would not undertake a task were he not sure that he could cope with it.

If the cap fit yu, wear it.
React to my remarks only if they pertain to you.

If yu can get free milk, no bother buy cow.
Those with ready access to charity should not be expected to practice self-reliance.

If you can' hear, yu mus' feel.
If a person rejects good advice, he must be prepared for the consequences.

If yu can' ketch Quaco, ketch 'im shu't.
If you cannot achieve your goal, take advantage of the nearest alternative.

If yu can' stan' an' bu'n, cut an' run.
If you are unable to withstand pressure, try to avoid difficult situations.
Version: *If you can't take the heat, leave the kitchen.*

If yu come fi drink milk, no count cow.
If you choose to enjoy somenoe's hospitality, you ought not to question the source of his income.

If yu cuss John Crow peel-head, turkey wi' vex.
If you criticize the faults of one person, those with similar faults will take offense.

If yu a dig pit fi smaddy, dig one fi you'self as well.
A warning that the ills you plan for others may well overtake you.

If yu done cross river, no call alligator long mout'.
Never invite new dangers unless you are in a safe position to handle them.

If yu eye deep, start cry early.
Those who begin a task with a handicap should strive harder and begin earlier than others.

If yu 'fraid o' eye you can' eat head.
It is advisable for one to eat food only with which one is comfortable.

If yu 'fraid o' frog, yu wi' run from crab.
A timid person will be alarmed even if there is no threat.

If yu give dawg food pon plate, 'im tek it put pon groun'.
One unaccustomed to the social graces will err when good manners are required.

If yu go a tumpa-foot dance, yu mus' dance tumpa-foot.
Version: When in Rome, do as the Romans do.

If yu han' inna de lion moun', tek time draw it out.
To stir up and opponent stronger than yourself is unwise. A withdrawal is better.

If yu have dawg fi bark, yu no need fi bark you'self.
If a task is assigned to someone he should be left to do his work without undue interference.

If yu have raw meat yu mus' look for fire.
A person with a problem must seek a solution, and not wait for others to help.

If yu hol' de blade, mine how yu draw de knife.
When you are vulnerable, you must be cautious in dealing with those who can hurt you.

If yu kill me bury me too.
Don't go halfway with favors.

If yu lie down with dawg, yu must get up wit' fleas.
If you keep bad company you will acquire their habits.

If yu live 'pon smaddy eye-top yu wi' fall off as dem wink.
Never depend on another person to take care of your business.
Develop some indepence

If yu love cow, yu mus' love calf.
If you are courting a woman, you should love her child as well.

If yu love de daughter, yu haffe love de modda.
When courting a girl, be particularly nice to her mother.

If yu mek yu bed hard, yu mus' lie in it.
If you create tough circumstances for yourself, you must be prepared to endure the consequences.

If yu nuh go a man fireside, yu no know how much firestick bwile 'im pot.
For an accurate account of an event, it is advisable to go to the source.

If yu nuh have door fi shut, shut yu mout'.
The poor should avoid getting into trouble with cheap talk.

If yu nuh have good fi say, say nothin'.
It is better to be silent than to be offensive.

If yu nuh ketch 'im inna de wheel, ketch im inna de jig.
If you can't succed in one way, you must try another.

If yu nuh mash ants, yu no know 'im have guts.
You will not know how angry a quiet person is until you hurt his feelings.

If yu no walk a night, yu no hear crab cough.
Satirical reference to one who boasts of his knowledge gained by traveling.

If yu nuh walk a night yu no know sey puss have cockeye.
Only in the dark you will see the light of a cat's eye.

You have to stay up late to know what happens at night.

If yu nyam egg, yu haffi bruk shell.
Sometimes you have to make sacrifices in order to get improvement.

If yu plant peas an' yu a pick corn, an' hear clear throat, run.
If you reap what you did not sow, you are stealing and should be wary of your action.

If yu plant peas, yu can' reap corn.
You cannot work toward one objective and expect to achieve another.

If yu play de fool, yu get de fool's pay.
Reward is dictated by deed.

If yu play wid fire, yu wi' get bu'n.
If you live dangerously, you will get hurt.

If yu put butter in a puss mout', 'im mus' lick it.
If you tempt a thief, you must expect to suffer losses.

If yu see everybody a run, tek yu time.
Following a crowd can lead to trouble.

If yu talk to a hog, yu mus' expec' a grunt.
Don't expect to get wisdom by talking to a fool.

If yu throw stone inna pig sty, de one wey bawl a him yu lick.
If you make accusations, the guilty, rather than the innocent, will protest.

If yu trabel, yu wi know whe' water walk go a punkin belly.
Travel broadens one's vision, knowledge and understanding.

If yu trousers short, wear long braces.
Make the best of every situation in which you find yourself.

If yu wan' fi know yu frien', lay dung a roadside play drunk.
A false friend will speak ill of you if he thinks you are not hearing his remarks.

If yu wan' fi eat roas' plantain, yu mus' satisfy fi bun yu finger.
Version: By the sweat of your brow, you shall eat bread.

If yu must lean, no lean pon wiss.
If you depend on someone, make sure that that person is reliable.

If yu wan' fi lif' load, you haffi ben dung.
To resolve a problem, one must get to the root of the matter.

If yu wan' good, yu nose mus' run.
Every fruitful endeavor demands *some* measure of sacrifice.

If yu wan' taste ole 'oman pepperpot, yu haffi scratch ole 'oman back.
You have to be nice to anyone from whom you expect a favor.

'Im can' mash ants.
Used describe a quiet, cautious person.

'Im coco roas' and butter.
He has no problem.

Im go in like Johnny cake and come out like dumplin'
He has made no progress despite all the exposure he has had.

'Im goin' on like cock o' the walk.
He is behaving like a king overseeing his subjects.

'Im no know what o'clock a strike.
He is totally unaware of what is going on around him.

'I m no lif' straw.
He has been idle.

'Im no wort' 'im ears full o' cold water
He is totally useless.

Is a hell of ting when dish towel become tablecloth.
This is used in reference to one who has suddenly risen to a position for which he is not equipped.
Version: *Cock-a-benny tu'n yellow-tail. (These are birds)*

Is me one you have strent' for?
A question often asked by a person who feels that he/she has been singled out for disciplinary action.

Is not because cow no have tongue why 'im nuh talk.
A silent man is not necessarily a man without knowledge.

Is not "who yu know", but "who know yu".
It is more than advantageous to be known by others than for you to know about others.

It mek mi head grow.
This one is commonly used to describe a moving experience.

J

Jamaica turkey does fly high.
The John Crow, despised by many because it feeds on rotten meat, flies high. The phrase is used to jeer the lowly man who puts on airs.

Jigger no care 'bout backra foot.
Chiggers will attack any foot, black or white; so misfortune might befall anyone.

John Crow no care fi Sunday morning.
John Crow does not observe the Sabbath.

John Crow seh 'im a dandy-man, but 'im put bald head fi mek fas' smaddy find fault.
Used in reference to someone who pretends that his shortcomings are matters of choice.

John Crow seh dat from the time man a chop down tree, 'im neva sleep a groun' yet.
God provides for all creatures, including the birds of the air.

Jump outta fryin' pan, you lan' inna fire.
Sometimes the situation to which you aspire is worse than the one you are experiencing.

K

Ketch yu length.
Have a good time.

L

Learn fi dance at home before yu dance abroad.
Test your skill before your friends, before going to strangers.

Let sleeping dawg lie.
Don't stir up a situation lest you be blamed for what may follow.

Lick him wher' him pants tear!
Advice as to how one may defeat an enemy. Play on his weakness!

Lie an' t'ief a fus cousin.
One who tells a lie is as bad as a thief.

Lie down wid dawg, yu git up wid flea.
If you keep bad company you will share their reputation.

Like a dog to his own vomit.
Used in reference to one who returns to a position that he previously rejected.

Like butter 'gainst sun.
Often used in to describe the easy loss of resources.

Like a kitchen without a knife, is a man without a wife.
This is a comment concerning the usefulness of a woman in the household.

Lilly billy-goat have beard and big bull no have none.
A person's importance should not be judged by his appearance.

Live fo' today! Tomorrow will take care of itself.
It is important to remain focused on the business of the day.

Live-well can' leave very-well alone.
Used in reference to one who is never satisfied to leave well enough alone.

Long road draw sweat, short-cut draw blood.
Better to use the proven route than take what appears to be an easier path.

Lucky bawn better dan well bred.
To be born lucky is better than to be well-trained.

M

Man a carry straw no fool wid fire.
Always be cautious when dealing with a delicate situation.

Man appoint, God disappoint.
Used in reference to man's fallability.

Man born fi heng can' drown.
One cannot escape one's destiny.

Man 'ceitful like a star-apple leaf.
Star-apple leaves are bronze on one side, green on the other.

Man cubbitch like star-apple.
No matter how ripe the star-apple is, it never falls from the tree.

Man hate yu, 'im gi yu basket fi carry water.
One who dislikes you will give you impossible tasks to perform.

Man ha' fi tek de will fi de deed sometimes.
Sometimes we have to judge a person by his intentions rather than his deeds.

Man nu dead nu call 'im duppy.
Never quit until all trials have failed.

Man talk too much, 'im pay 'im puppa debt.
Too much meddling can put one in serious trouble.

Man wey tie mad dawg a de right smaddy fi loose 'im.
A job is best entrusted to one whose skill is already proven.

Man who no tell lie have hair inna 'im hand middle.
It is impossible to find one who has never told a lie.

Many ways fi hang dawg widdout puttin' a rope to im neck
There are many ways of getting revenge.

Marriage 'ave teet', and sometime teet, get toot'ache.
Married life is not as carefree as single life.

Mash up de dolly house.
Used to describe trouble caused by exposing business deals.

Massa horse, massa grass.
There is no harm if the master's horse eats the master's grass.

Massy, mi massa!
Lord, have mercy!

Mawga cow a still prize bull mumma.
Success cannot change a person's origin.

Mawga dawg can' pass ole bone.
A starving person cannot refuse any kind of food.

Mek 'im play 'im own music and dance to it.
This is one way of saying 'ignore him'.

Mek yu belly talk more dan yu mouth.
Sometimes it is better to moan than to disclose what your heart feels.

Mek smaddy long fi see yu.
This is an advice not to visit a person too often.

Mi beg but mi don' sponge.
I will ask for help but not humiliate myself in so doing.

Mi eye is mi market.
I won't buy unless my eyes are satisfied with the goods.

Mi live fi see san'fly tek crowbar dig jigger outta mosquito foot.
Used in reference to an occurrence that seemed impossible.

Mi nuh have big pot fi bwile belly gut.
I am incapable of handling that task.
Version: *Mi nuh have blue boot fi go clim' eleven step'.*

Mi nuh talk wid water inna me mouth.
This is the testimony of an outspoken person.

Mi t'row mi corn, mi nuh call no fowl.
Rebuke to one who reacts to remarks that were not directed specifically to him.

Money mek de mare run.
One performs better when there are incentives.

Money nu grow pon tree.
One must spend money wisely, as it cannot be picked from trees.

More rain, more res'.
Outdoor workers get more opportunitie to rest whenever it rains.

More dan John read 'bout.
More than enough.

Mosquito nuh trouble deaf ears people.
What you can't hear won't bother you.

Muzzle dawg can' ketch rat.
A person cannot perform well without the necessary tools or authority.

N

Nanny-goat nuh scratch 'im back till 'im see wall.
Timing is important in taking action.

Near neighbor better tha' far bredda.
Better to have a good friend nearby than a relative far away.

Nearly never kill bud.
To have almost attained an objective is not the same as reaching the target.

Needle mek clothes, but needle naked.
Some tend to look about other people's business while neglecting their own.

Nevva buy puss in bag.
Be sure to check a product or proposal before accepting it.

Nevva see, come see.
This is made in reference to someone who is enjoying circumstances to which he/she is unaccustomed.

New broom sweep clean, but ole broom know de corners.
A situation is best dealt with by those who are familiar with it.

No' everyt'ing good to eat, good to talk.
A person should know when to remain silent and not divulge information he may have.

No' everyt'ing wit' sugar taste sweet.
All that glitters is not gold.

Not'ing beat a failure but a trial.
You can't be too sure that you will fail unless you try.

Not'ing done before the time.
In life there is a time for everything.

Not'ing tried, not'ing done.
You can't be sure that you will succed unless you try.
Anyone who is unwilling to try will never experience the joy of accomplishment.

Nuh better herrin', no better barrel.
Thi describes two of a kind.

Nuh bite off more dan yu can chew.
Never take on more than you can comfortably manage.

Nuh cut no track fi monkey.
Don't give help to one not deserving of it.
Version: *No fatten cockroach fi fowl.*

Nuh gi wey you ass and shit through yu ribs.
Advice not to deprive yourself of essentials in order to please others.

Nuh hang yu hat higher than yu can reach it.
Don't set yourself unrealistic goals or undertake debts which you can ill afford.

Nuh put puss fi watch butter.
Never tempt a person who has a weakness for taking things.

Nuh rain, nuh rainbow.
You cannot enjoy the beauty of the rainbow without getting the inconvenience of rain.

Nuh sankey nuh sing so!
This is not right! Sankey is the name given to certain religious tunes written by a songwriter with that name.

Nuh swap black black dawg fi monkey.
The folly of exchanging one situation for another that is no better.
Version: *Six of one, half dozen of the other.*

Nuh tek it mek habit.
Admonition to persons always asking favors.

Nuh tek it put pon yu head.
Don't let it worry you.

Nuh waste powder pon blackbud.
Don't try to change something that cannot be changed.

Nyanga mek crab go sideways.
This is a reference to those who put on airs to make an impression.

O

Oil and water can' mix.
People from different social standings do not make good partners

Ol' fiddie play new tune.
This Indicates a change of mind.

Ol' firestick easy fi ketch.
This illustrates how very easy it is for two old lovers to renew their relationship.

On 'is uppers.
Used to describe someone so badly off that he/she cannot mend his/her shoes.

On the bones of 'is ass.
Used to describe someone down and out, and experiencing hard times.

Once a man twice a chil'.
One who gets old often needs as much assistance as child.

One day busha a busha.
This is used in reference to one who has once acted in a position of authority, but continues to exercise the bearing of his former office.

One-eye man a king inna blind-eye country.
Used to describe one with limited knowledge leading others more limited than he is.

One fool makes many.
A fool will makes a fool of all who follow his example.

One han' can' kill mosquito.
At times a single occupation will not bring enough income to satisfy one's needs.
Version: *One han' can' clap.*

One han' wash de other.
By helping a person, one ensures that he will be assisted in return.

One one coco full basket.
A little at a time will still get the job done.

One pumpkin worry basket.
One pumpkin in a basket will keep rolling and tossing as the carrier goes along. A full basket is easier to balance.

One smaddy can' quarrel.
Version: *It takes two to make a quarrel.*

One time is accident, but two times is habit.
Used in reference to making mistakes.

Only de man who wear de shoes can tell yu where it pinch.
No one can experience physical pain for another.

Order monkey, monkey order 'im tail.
Give a man orders and he will, in turn, order his child.

P

'Panna machete cut both ways.
Like a Spanish machete, some people will play both sides.

Parson christen 'im pickney fus.
A person takes care of his own before looking after others.

Patience is a virtue; too much of it will hurt you.
One should exercise patience but not allow every opportunity to pass while waiting.

Patient man ride jackass.
This speaks to the advantage of acting in a timely manner.
Version: *Hol' on to yu brush.*

Peacock hide 'im foot when 'im hear bout 'im tail.
Some are like the peacock that has a beautiful tail but ugly feet.

Pickney nyam mumma. but mumma nuh nyam pickney.
Parents show more kindness to children than vice versa.

Pickeny we talk too much pay 'im mumma an' puppa debts.
A talkative child will expose family secrets.

Pig ask 'im mumma wha' mek 'im mout' so long. De mumma sey, "No mine, yu a grow, yu wi' fin' out".
If one cannot learn by observation, he will learn by personal experience.

Pipe nuh care who stan' up back a it.
The pipe doesn't care who the smoker is, because it is always in front.

Plait san' an' stone breeze.
This describes the occupation of an idler.

Plantain wha' ripe can' green again.
When a person gets old, he cannot be young again.

Play fool fi ketch wise.
Sometimes you have to pretend to be confused in order to decieve the wise.

Play stone kill bud.
Sometimes one may hit the target without intending to.

Play wid puppy, puppy lick yu mout'.
Familiarity breeds contempt.

Plenty han's mek work light.
A task becomes easier when others help.

Poor ketch Cubba 'im tun sarvant fi dawg.
In times of great need, one has to take any kind of job.

Poor show great.
This is a reference to false pride, when one boasts without having anything proof to justify the boast.

Poppy-show hav' dem gang.
Even fools have their supporters.

Pop story gi mi!
Give me some news!

Pot can' call kettle black.
One should not criticize faults that one has oneself.

Pot full, de cover get some.
When a man has plenty, his friends are likely to share his property.

Poun' a fret never pay quattie wort' a debt.
A lot of fretting without action will not solve any problems.

Pretty feather no mek pretty bud.
A colorful bird can sometimes be a cross bird.

Puppy done nyam ratta, 'im cut capoose pon John Crow.
Early success often leads one to overrate one's capabilities.

Puss and dawg no have de same luck.
Not everyone can do the same thing and get away with it.

Puss belly full, 'im say pear have skin.
When a man is satisfied, he can afford to criticize the source of his supply.
Version: *When puss belly full, 'im say ratta tail stink.*

Puss bruk coconut inna you eye.
Used as a rebuke to a bare-faced person.

Puss gone rat tek charge.
When those in charge are absent, others have their own way.

Puss no business inna dog fight.
Outsiders should stay clear of family feuds.

Puss siddung a marketgate a laugh after dawg distress.
Used in reference to one who mocks the unfortunate rather than gives a helping hand.

Put a beggar pon a horse, 'im ride himself to hell.
Promote a person to a position for which he is not qualified and he will destroy himself.

Q

Quart pot tu'n down, gill pot tu'n up.
Adults are quiet, children noisy.

Quattie buy trouble, hundred poun' can' cure it.
It is easy to get into trouble but very hard to get out of it.

Quick ninepence better dan slow shillin'.
A little help in time is better than a lot coming too late.

R

Rain a fall but dutty tough.
In the best of times, there are some who will still experience hardships.

Rain fall 'pon all a wi.
God has no favorites. He is good to all mankind.

Rest pon mi chest.
Used in rference to food that has not been digested.

Rockstone a river bottom no know sun hot.
It is difficult for those born and reared in comfort to understand the difficulties of the poor.

S

Same knife stick sheep, stick goat.
The same difficulty that confronts one person can also confront his friends.

Scornful dawg nyam dutty puddin'.
A dog will leave a good meal and yet eat garbage.

See an' blin', hear an' deaf.
Used as a warning not to speak about anything heard or seen.

See de candlelight befor' yu blow out de match.
Version: No throw 'way dutty water before yu have clean one.

See me an' come live wid me Is two different t'ings.
It is only by living with a person that you can know his true character.

Self-praise is no recommendation.
Even a bad workman will praise his own skills.

Sen' bwoy go call doctor, doctor come before bwoy.
This makes reference to a tardy person.

Sen' out pickney, yu foot rest, but yu heart tired.
Send your child on an errand and you worry about his safety until he returns.

Sensay fowl no want fedda, 'im want corn.
Food is better than raiment.

Seven year nevva too long fi wash speckle off a guinea-hen back.
This is a warning that a person will not easily forget or forgive an injury.

Shake yu tail accordin' to yu size.
Know your place and act accordingly.

Shame a no weight, but it bruk neck.
Shame can make a person hang his head so low it appears that his neck is broken.

She/he get up on the wrong side o' de bed dis morning.
Used in reference to someone who got up in the morning in a bad mood.

Show me yu company, a tell yu who yu are.
One's character is often judged by the company one keeps.

Show yu ten commandments.
Expose your bare feet and ten toes.

Shut mout' no ketch fly.
This is an advice to mind your own business.

Sick a laugh after dead.
This is an observation of a fallen one being mocked by one not far from falling himself.

Sickness ride horse fi come, but tek foot fi go.
It takes a shorter time to become ill than to become well again.

Siddung nevva sa' git-up.
One never wants to get up when he is comfortably seated and enjoying the company.

Silver dollar better than fambly.
Money in the pocket is more comforting than faraway relatives.

Since Wappy kill Phillup.
Used in reference to a long, long time ago.

Sleep no hav' no massa.
No one can fight sleep when it comes.

Small axe fall big tree.
A person's size bears no relationship to his ability to tackle a task.

Snake bite yu, yu run when yu see lizard.
Version: Once bitten, twice shy.

Soap and water no 'fraid fe dutty clothes
If corrective action is taken, a turn around is possible in the worst of situations.

Softly river run deep.
A quiet person is usually a deep thinker.

Solja blood but gineral name.
The soldier does the fighting but the general gets the fame.

Somet'ing ina somet'ing.
Something funny is going on.

Sometimes coffee, sometimes tea.
One must accept change and not expect that things will be the same at all times.

Sometimes standin' collar stan' top a empty belly.
Used in reference to those who pretend to be better off than they really are.

So mi get it, a so mi sell it!
I have given a true account, with nothing added or subtracted.

Sorry fi mawga dawg, mawga dawg tu'n roun' bite yu.
Help given to a needy person is sometimes repaid with ingratitude.

Spare de rod an' spwile de chile.
A child who is not punished for wrongdoing will grow up to be unruly.

Spider an' fly can' mek bargain.
Two sworn enemies cannot make a satisfactory agreement.

Spit in de sky, it fall inna yu face.
Rudeness to your superiors can bring unwelcome humiliation.

Stan' an' look can' spwile dance.
Assuming a neutral position will not make a situation worse.

Stan' pon crooked an' cut straight.
Even if conditions are not ideal, the good workman should try for the highest standard of performance.

Stan' softly better dan beg pardon.
It is better not to cause offense than having to apologize.
***Version:** Tek care better dan beg pardon.*

Stranger no fi walk a back door.
A stranger should not pry into family matters.

Strong man never wrong.
In any endeavor, the weak cannot defeat the strong.

Story come to bump.
The time of reconing is here!

Sturdiration beat education.
One who studies life is wiser than one who only reads about it.

Suck salt through a wooden spoon.
This means to experience hard times.

Sugar barrel never mash ants.
The source of pleasure cannot be blamed for one's overindulgence.

Sweet mout' mek fly follow coffin go a hole.
Flattery will lead a man to his grave.

Sweet soup mek man drink ants.
Pleasurable activities sometimes lead to sorrow.

T

Teet' and tongue must meet.
It is normal for people who live together to have differences.

Tek bad sinting mek laugh.
This is an advice to keep good humor in the face of adversity.

Tek kin teeth cover heart burn.
An advice regarding the use a smile to cover inward pain.

Tek sleep an' mark death.
One should try to profit from the experiences of others.

Ten suit a tailor better dan one suit a law.
Used in reference to the problems regarding a trial in a court of law.

Tief no like see 'nother tief carry long bag.
Even a thief does not like to see his competitor succeed.

Time longer dan rope.
One must exercise patience, knowing that time is eternal.

Time never too long fi bannabis bear.
The banner bean takes a long time to bear. So a person is advised to be patient.

Time so hard dat dawg an all a look work.
Difficulties will make a person do unusual things.

Time spanner fit every bolt.
With time, all problems can be solved.

Today fi mi, tommorrow fi yu.
The burden I suffer today may be yours tommorrow.

Tom drunk but Tom no fool.
A man may be drunk, and yet acts instinctively to protect his interests.

Too much a one t'ing god for nuttin'.
Repitition leads to boredom.

Too much cousin bruk shop.
Too many members of the family in the shop will lead to bankruptcy because each will expect something for nothing.

Too much ratta never dig good hole.
If you put too many persons on a job, there is likely to be confusion and poor results.

Too much siddung wear out trousers.
A lazy man will never have money to replace his clothes.

Trouble de a bush, Anansi tek it bring home.
Some people go out of their way to get into trouble.

Trouble mek ole 'oman trot.
Even the feeble will work if circumstances dictate it.

Trouble no set like rain.
Trouble seldom gives notice.

Trouble tek yu, pickney shu't fit yu.
In times of difficulty, a man will take any help he can get.

Truth like oil mus' swim.
The truth will inevitably overcome lies.

Turkey can' call John Crow peel head.
One with a shortcoming cannot criticize another with the same fault.

Two bull' can' reign inna one pen.
Two persons of string wills cannot share authority.

Two head better dan one, if it is even coco head.
A second opinion is useful even if the advisor has limited experience.

Two jackass can' bray one time.
Advice to one speaker who is interrupting another.

U

Ungrateful worse than obeah.
The consequences of ingratitude is worst than witchcraft.

W

Wait kill man.
Response by an impatient person asked to wait. There's a play here on the word *weight.*

Walk 'bout potato never bear.
A potato vine running wild never bears.
Version: *A rolling stone gathers no moss.*

Walk fi nutten better dan siddung fi nutten.
One is likely to achieve more by going out than by sitting at home.

Wall 'ave ears and bush 'ave eye.
It is difficult to keep a secret even when one stays behind walls or in the bushes.

Want all? Loose all.
The person who tries to take all, usually end up loosing all.

Wash smaddy pickney belly, but n' wash 'im back.
Don't go all out to help somebody's child, lest the child becomes ungrateful.

Wass-wass buil' comb, but 'im can' put fat inna it.
This is used in reference to one who starts a job but cannot complete it it.

Water more than flour.
Alluding to someone experiencing hardships and inconveniences.

Water nevva run uphill.
Because of reputation, there are some things that a person is not expected to do.

We no plant gungu a line.
This describes and instance of two neighbors who are not on friendly terms.

Wha' de use yu a shawl up when yu character gone.
A beautiful dress cannot conceal a bad character.

Wha' drop off a pickney head fall pon puppa shoulder.
A father is often held responsible for his children's behavior.

Wha' eye no see, heart no leap for.
One does not hanker for something one does not know.

Wha' fall off a head, drop pon shoulder.
What a man does not need, he passes it on to his nearest relative or friend.

Wha' gone bad a morning, can' come good a evening.
When a job begins badly, it cannot be right at the end.

Wha' nayga sey; if a no so, a nearly so it go.
There is some truth in every rumour.

Wha' no dead, no dash 'way.
Be frugal. Don't discard anything that can be of use.

Wha' stay too long serve two master.
If you wait too long to make use of an opportunity, someone else might take it.

Wha' sweet nanny goat always run 'im belly.
Pleasures often end in pain.

Watch pot neva boil.
Too much over-supervision can interfere with performance.

What gone bad a mornin' can't come good a night.
A task poorly begun cannot be successful in the end.

What you don't know older dan yu.
One cannot make use of something that one does not understand.

What is fi yu can' be unfi yu.
What you are destined to receive will eventually come to you.

What is joke to yu is death to mi.
Version: One man's meat is another man's poison.

What monkey have, is what 'im giv' 'm frien'.
Friends are always willing to share.

What no dead nuh dash wey.
An advice to make use of everything that you own until it is no longer serviceable.

What never happen in a year, happen in a day.
Something unexpected suddenly occurs.

What yu can' cure, you mus' endure.
If you cannot solve a problem, you should learn to live with it.

What you get is not always what you want.
No one can dictate the gifts of God.

When belly full, jaw mus' stop.
Version: *Enough is enough.*

When black man tief, 'im tief half a bit; when backra tief, 'im tief de whole estate.
This phrase was often used in the days following slavery.

When bull begin fi dig grung, yu better look fi tree.
When yu see trouble, better find a way to escape.

When bull ole, yu tek hog meat tie 'im.
The strong can be humiliated when they become old.

When cockroach gi party, 'im no ask fowl.
One should not keep company with one's enemies.

When cocoa ripe 'im mus' bus'.
Used in reference to one who makes a big display and then comes to grief.

When cow tail cut off, God Almighty brush fly fi 'im.
The good Lord will take care of those who are in need of assistance.

When fly bodder mawga mule, nobody no see; but when 'im kick, dem say 'im bad.
A person is often criticized when he retaliates.

Wen fowl drink water, 'im say,"T'ank God!" When man drink water 'im say nutten.
Fowl lift their heads as they drink and this is taken to mean thanks to the Almighty.

When fowl grabel 'im pickney, 'im no tell hawk fi pick it up.
A parent scolds his child but resents anyone else doing so.

When fowl have teet'!
That will be the day!

When fum-fum come, story come.
The threat of a beating brings out the truth.

When goat foot bruck, im fin' im yard.
A wayward child will return to the home when disaster strikes.

When jackass dead, bees tek 'im backbone mek honey.
Every object has some use.

When man belly full, 'im bruk pot.
This is a sign of ingratitude.

When man git up wid waistcoat Monday morning, you know 'im shut back tear.
Waistcoats were once expected to be worn only on Sundays, unless the wearer was covering up his shirt.

When man 'ave coco-head in a barrel, 'im can go pick up wife.
An independent person can afford to undertake responsibilities.

When man live well, 'im go a paster go tell cow howdy.
Version: The devil finds work for idle hands.

When man no done grow, 'im never shoulda cuss long man.
An adolescent should not comment adversly on an adult's statue since he does not know what his future holds.

When mango season plenty, nayga stoccado wear black pot.
When mangoes are plentiful, the cooking pot is not used much.

When pear tree fall, puss laugh.
Disaster for one can be a blessing for another.

When plantain wan' dead, 'im shoot.
The plaintain dies after it bears; so does a person who courts disaster by provoking others.

When puss an' dawg nyam togedda, de bickle belong to puss.
Because the cat is weaker, the dog is not expected to share his food with the cat.

When ratta bite bottle, calabash mus' run.
If a strong man falls, the weak must try to get away.

When six eye meet, story done.
When a third person joins two gossipers, the stories are brought to an end.

When tiger wan' nyam 'im pickney, 'im say 'im favor puss.
A man will make any excuse to justify his conduct.

When two dawg fight fi bone, neither dawg tek it 'way.
A third party sometimes benefits from a struggle between two persons.

When yu se' ole 'Oman run, no ask wha' matter, run too.
If a situation dictates desperation, act quickly to avoid them.

When yu se' shit, walk over it, nuh inna it.
When you see trouble, always try to avoid it.

When yu se' sickness, don't rule out death.
Sickness should be a constant reminder of death.

When yu se' yu neighbor beard ketch fire, tek water wet fi yu.
Let your friend's predicament be a sign for you to be prepared for similar trouble.

When yu visit donkey house, no talk 'bout ears.
Be careful how you make criticism in the presence of those who may be offended.

Where dogs are not invited, bones are not provided.
Uninvited guests should not expect their preferences to be addressed.

Where you bound, you must obey.
It is wise to be faithful, especially when you have no choice in the matter.

Whey de use yu da shawl up when yu character gone?
A beautiful dress cannot conseal a bad character.

Whey yu been deh when blackbud was a holler?
Where were you when there were opportunities to better yourself.?

Who have fingernail no have itch; who have itch no have fingernail.
Some people have assets for which they have no need but which would be useful to others.

Woman luck deh a dungle.
No matter how down and out a woman may be, there is always the chance that she will meet someone to look after her.

Wonder what all like 'im gwine tell God sey?
Wonder what account will he be able to give of himself on judgement day?
This is usually used in reference to someone whose behavior is reprehensible.

Willin' horse get saddle de mos'.
There is more work for one who demonstrates a willingness to work without complaint.

Y

Yerry say can' go a law.
Hearsay is not admissible in a court of law and should be discounted in any discussion.

Yes, yes never carry man over mountain.
Words alone cannot solve problems.

Yu can lead a horse to water, but yu can' mek 'im drink.
There is a limit to the possibility of motivating an unwilling person.

Yu haffe mash ants fi fin' him guts.
It is only when hurt, that some people will speak out.

Yu can' hide from a tief but not from a liar.
Version: He who steals my purse steals trash, but he who robs me of my good name, makes me poor indeed.

Yu can' learn fi fly if yu no leave nes'.
One can only prove independence by acting without the help of others.

You can' hide bush fire with smoke.
There is a limit to which explosive matters can be kept secret.

Yu can' mek blood outta stone.
You cannot make something out of nothing.

Yu can' stay pon cow back an' cuss cow skin.
You should not be rude to someone upon whom you are dependent.

Yu can' tek narri sommari eye so sleep.
Self-reliance is beter than depending upon others.
(narri sommari - next somebody)

Yu can' top bud from fly, but yu can prevent dem from pitch pon yu head.
One may not be able to stop wrongdoing, but one can try to avoid it.

Yu coco roas' an' butter!
You have nothing to worry about!

Yu don' know what o'clock a strike.
You are unaware of the danger that threatens.

Yu fan fly, yu hurt sore.
Good intentions often make matters worse.

Yu haffi kiss ass before yu can kick it.
You can outwit the strong man by letting him think you are weak.

Yu in de right church, but de wrong pew.
You are half-right and half-wrong.

Yu never se' kickin' cow widout kickin' calf.
The offspring always follow the parent.

Yu never se' smoke widout fire.
Some signs are very reliable. For instance, smoke cannot be produced unless there is fire.

Yu se' man face, yu nuh se' 'im heart.
You cannot tell a man's true feelings by the look on his face.

Yu se' today, yu nuh se' tomorrow.
You may be sure of what is happening today, but remember that the future is uncertain.

Yu tek the word right outo' mi mouth.

This is used when the speaker's conversation is interrupted by another who verbalizes the precise words that the speaker would have used, had he not been interrupted.

Yu think me only use me head fi block hat?

Among other things, I use my head to think.

FROM OTHER CARIBBEAN LANDS

BARBADOS

A eyefyl en' a bellyful.
Seeing is one thing, having it in your possession is another thing. This has sexual overtones.

A shoemaker wife foot always at de door. *("At the door" means exposed, because of holes in the shoes).*
Skilled workmen seldom take time off to use their skills for personal advantage.

Better fish in de sea dan wha' ketch.
There is always someone who will make a better lover than the current one.

Common dog does bark in church.
Uncivilized individuals will conduct themselves in an uncouth manner irrespective of the situation.

De higher de monkey climb, de more 'e show 'e tail.
The more you show off the more your faults are brought to the open.

De sea en' got nuh back door.
The sea is not a safe place since there is no gurantee that you will get back out.

Dirty water does cool hot iron.
Once aroused, almost any woman, whether good or bad, can quench a man's lust.

Donkey have long ear, but 'e don' like to hear 'e own story.
People do not like to hear or accept their own faults.

Evah bush is man.
Be careful how you talk, as you never know who is listening.

Evah fool got 'e sense.
Everybody is knowledgeable in one area or the other, no matter how dull or ignorant he or she may seem.

Gih Jack 'e jacket.
Give every man his credit.

High wind know wih ole house live.
Advantage is taken of those known to be weak.

Hold de light fuh de devil tuh sih, an when yuh get a chance, blow it out in 'e face.
Ahen you know that somebody has bad intentions but is pretending they mean well, you should play along with them unti the opportunity comes when you can foil his plans.

Home drum beat first.
Before taking on someone else's problems, you should first look after your family interests.

Lime juice can' spoil vinegar.
An individual can't be corrupted by another who is less corrupt.

Loose goat don't know wha' tie goat sih (see).
One has to be in someone else's shoe in order to understand what he is going through.

Never eat and forget.
Never forget the hands that feed you.

Never wuk groun' fuh monkey run pon.
You should never exert great energy on a venture knowing that some unworthy person will benefit.

News don' lack a carrier.
There is always someone ready to spread anthing newsworthy, especially if it is gossip.

Ole coachman nevah forget de snap o' de whip.
One rarely forgets a skill which one has learnt and practiced over a long time

One-one blow kill ole cow.
What may seem like a trivial irritation may create a catastrophy if repeated often enough.

One smart dead at two smart door.
No matter how smart you think you are, there is somebody smarter than you

Play wid puppy an' puppy lick yuh mout'.
To be familiar to those of a lower status creates an atmosphere for them to treat you with scant respect.

The higher de monkey climb, de more 'e show 'e tail.
The more you show off, the more your faults are brought to the open.

Two smart rat can' live in de same hole.
Two tricksters cannot get along with each other.

Yuh can' put mangoose tuh watch chicken.
Never trust people with things which will be a great temptation to them.

Yuh can' stop yuh ear from hearing, but uh can stop yuh mouth from talking.
A warning against repeating what one has heard.

Yuh should sell yuh butter whi yuh get yuh lard.

Bet who bet yuh.
Help those who help you.

When a bird fly too fast, 'e fly past 'e nest.
Being over ambitious has its drawbacks.

When yuh en' got horse, ride cow.
Utilize whatever resources you have available

BELIZE

Bad ting nevva got owner.
Nobody takes responsibility for wrong doings.

Blow yu nose same place yu ketch yu cold.
When adversity comes, turn to your friends, especially if they contributed to your misfortune.

Buy today. Credit tomorrow.
Buy. Never credit. Tomorrow never comes.

Come fus tek.
Those who are early have the advantage over those who are not.

De water tase sweetest at de head a di stream.
For the best results, deal with the person at the top.

Fisherman nevva sey e fish stink.
Do not expect a person to bare his own faults.

Fish get ketch by e mouth.
Be careful of loose talk.

Food weh no killing, fattening.
Don't make a fuss about food.

Fool-fool man kill cow fa wise man eat.
It is easy for a fool to become a prey of the wise.

Gaad no like ugly.
Injustice will not prevail.

Good looking and good luck no always walk di same road.
Beauty does not guarantee success.

Hol' on to weh yu have an' grab fa more.
A proverbial challenge never to give up on acquiring more.

If crab no walk e no get fat. If e walk too much e lose e claw.
All experiences in life involve a certain degree of risk.

Liad enough to lie Jesus Christ off the cross.
A proverbial description of a liar.

Man da waak, ded di watch am.
Death awaits every man.

No call alligator long mout till yu done cross di rivva.
Don't insult anyone who has the power to hurt you.

No put puss fa min' butter
Don't tempt a thief.

One plate a dinna no fatten mawga daag.
It takes more than one act to rehabilitate an outcast.

Trouble neva meck eself.
A proverbial warning to stay out of trouble.

W

Wen rain come, dutty slippery.
A proverbial description of hard times.

GUYANA

All cassava gat same skin, but all nah taste same way.
Though people may look alike because of their mode of dress,
they are different in their ways.

All *shut eye* nah sleep.
Beware of pretences.

Big tree fall down, goat bite he leaf.
When a great man falls, he is no longer feared and respected.

Chicken got feddah, but he can't do fowl wuk.
Youth has its limitations. Experience teaches wisdom.

Dog foot bruck, he know he massa door.
In times of trouble we return to the comfort of our families.

Dog wha use to suck egg caan lef off.
Said in reference to one who is unable to overcome a bad habit.

Don't take *sham-face* an shake ku-ku-beh (leprosy) man han.
Don't let pride tempt you to do something you may later regret.

Drunk man tell lanter post "Ah beg yu pardon sah"
A drunkard hallucinates at times.

Drunk, or sober, mind your number.
There is no excuse for being unmannerly.

Easy lesson good fuh dunce.
Simple information to satisfy a simple mind.

Every rope got two ends.
Every story has two sides.

Family cutlish don't cut deep.
Family members do not remain annoyed with each other for a long time.

Far better fu see thing a daytime, than fuh take *firestick* look fuh it a nightime.
Seize an opportunity whenever it arrives.

Fool ah talk, but nah fool ah listen.
A wise person detects the short falls of one who thinks he is wise.

Greedy man does vex twice.
A person who is usually annoyed to share what he has, is also annoyed when others refuse to share with him.

Hand wash hand make hand come clean.
One act of kindness deserves another.

If oil ah float, watah deh ah battam.
A little evidence can tell the whole story.

If yuh mek yuself grass, horse guh eat yu.
When we respect ourselves, we gain the respect of others.

If yuh eye no see, yuh mouth nah must talk.
You must see for yourself before you talk.

If yuh nuh got mumma, yu got fuh suck granny.
Learning to make do with what is available.

If yuh see yu matie a jump pon one foot, yu jump pon one foot too.
An advice regarding flexibility.

If she good fuh breakfast, she must be good fuh dinner.
If a woman is good enough for a close relationship with a man, she should be good enough to be his wife.

It nuh good to shove yuh foot in every stocking.
You should not try to position yourself everywhere, or in everthing.

Man a pint; God a gallon.
God is superior to man.

Moon a run 'til day catch 'am.
A fugitive will eventually be caught.

Mouth-ar nah giutar.
Talk is cheap, action is not.

Mouth open, 'tory jump out.
The more we talk, the more we expose what is in our minds.

More deh in the mortar than the pestle.
Often there is more to a situation than meets the eye.

Mumma dead, fambly done.
In most families, members do not maintain a close relationship after the passing of the mother.

Nah every crabhole gat crab.
Things do not always trun out to be what you expect.

Never eat yu bread you one.
It is a good practice to share with the needy.

Rain fall at everybody door, but not at the same time.
No one is immune to trouble.

Rain nah full am. Dew caan full am.
It is not a wise practice to waste valuable studying time, hoping to make up for it at the last minute.

***Stan so*ftly better than *beg pardon*.**
It is wise to avoid an unpleasant situation by saying nothing.

Stranger nuh know burying ground.
A stranger is usually unaware of existing pitfalls.

Thief from thief mek God laugh.
It is regarded as amusing when one gets a taste of his own medicine.

Though poor, nuh show poor.
One should avoid showing one's adverse circumstances to the world.

When a loose mi bull in the pasture, yu better pen up yu heifer.
I am not responsible for the amorous actions of my son.

When fust bill ring nobody take notice.
The beginning of something unpleasant is often ignored until it escalates.

When yu si yu matie house a bun, throw water.
Help your friend when there is a crisis.

When yu own louse bite yu, he propper hut yu.
The pain is greater when our own relatives hurt us.

HAITI

A bird in the hand is better than two in the bushes.
This is a case of choosing certainty over uncertainty.

A one-eyed man is king in the world of the blind.
This   underscores the important part one can play, dispite his/her handicap.

All food is fit to eat, but not all words are fit to speak.
While one should be careful about the food one eats, one should be even more careful obout the words one speaks.

Age and marriage tame the beast.
These are two situations in life that often bring about a change for the better.

A monkey never thinks her baby is ugly.
All mothers think that their babies are beautiful.

An ounce of prevention is better tha a pound of cure.
It is better to prevent than to heal.

A single finger cannot catch fleas.
Cooperation makes any job easier.

Better rags than nakedness.
It is far better to be ragged and dirty, than to be naked.

Birds of a feather flock together.
People with similar traits tend to forge lasting relationships.

Beyond the mountain is another mountain.
Where there is a problem, be aware that another may not be too far away.

Eggs have no business dancing with stones.
It is wise to steer clear of known enemies.

He who steals an egg will steal a cow.
A thief will steal anything, regardless of its size.

Ignorance doesn't necessarily kill you, but it does make you sweat a lot.
Some things may not you kill you, but can cause you some discomfort.

In love, there is always one who kisses and one who offers the cheek.
Love is a two - way street.

The donkey sweats so that the horse can be decorated with lace.
The donkey is expected to do the hard work, but the horse is not.

The child of a tiger, is a tiger.
A child usually bears the traits of his/her mother

The pencil of God has no eraser.
God never makes a mistake.

There is always sunshine after the rain.
There may be hardships, but they must come to an end sooner or later.

If someone sweats for you, you change his shirt.
One good turn deserves another.

If work was good for you, the rich would leave none for the poor.
This speaks to the usual selfish nature of most rich people.

Edna Bennett

It is better to bend than to break.
This speaks to the need to be flexible when the situation demands it.

It is better to prevent than to heal.
Version: An ounce of prevention is better than a pound of cure.

No pillow is as soft as a clear conscience.
Peace of mind is the product of a clear concsience.

You cannot make omlettes without breaking the eggs.
To be successful, one has to be prepared to make sacrifices.

You cannot teach monkeys to make faces.
Version: You cannot teach old dogs new tricks.

When we cannot get what we love, we must love what is within our reach.
In life it is wise to be flexible.

Where there is no faith, there can be no miracles.
Version: Belief kills and belief cures.

Write injuries in sand, but benefits in marble.
The advice here is to put our failures behind us and focus on our successes

ST. KITTS/NEVIS

Day run 'till night catch him.
A person can do whatever he likes, but not for as long as he likes.

God don't like ugly.
God does not like ugly deeds and He will punish them.

Good Callallou don't make a good wife.
Just because something looks god, it does not mean it is so.

Head mek book. Book tun roun' puzzle head.
Although many men write books, there are many men who cannot read.

If yu think dat all *skin teet'* is a joke, guh look at the last person they bury.
Not all smiles are genuine.

Time longer than twine.
Time is eternal. Twine is not.

Until the wind blow, yuh never realy see fowl bottom (behind).
In a crisis a person's true personality surfaces.

What monkey see monkey does.
Some people always follow what others do.

Who have de watch keep de look out.
Each worker must perform according to his assigned role.

TRINIDAD AND TOBAGO

All skin teeth ain't smile.
All smiles are not true.

Dog don't make cat.
Children are always like their parents.

Don't pray to live with yu aunt.
An aunt is no substitute for a mother.

Edna Bennett

Eat little and live long.
Don't be greedy like some contractors. Negotiate, bid lower, grab the job.

Every pig has their Sunday.
Each of us will have our day of reckoning.

Hurry birds don't build good nest.
Often said in reference to speedy mariages.

Man da waak, ded di watch am.
Death awaits every man.

Monkey know what tree to climb.
People who are up to no good know who to interfere with.

Moon goes until daylight catch up with him.
People who do wrong will eventually meet justice.

No call alligator long mout till yu done cross di rivva.
Don't insult anyone who has the power to hurt you.

No put puss fa min' butter
Don't tempt a thief.

One plate a dinna no fatten maga dawg.
It takes more than one act to rehabilitate an outcast.

Put water in yu wine chile.
A call for a child to tone down his activity.

She mek she eat de bread de devil knead.
She makes life for her enemy miserable.

The longest rope have end and the longest prayer have amen.
Nothing lasts forever.

The small change in the pocket is what make the noise.
The simple is more talkative than the wise.

Trouble nevva meck eself.
A proverbial warning to stay out of trouble.

You can't play sailor and 'fraid powder'.
You must face the consequences of you actions.

Watch pot don' boil water.
Standing idly by does not get the job done.

Wen rain come, dutty slippery.
A proverbial description of hard times.

Wen yu si yu neighbor's house on fire, wet yu own.
When there are signs of impending danger, take action to avoid it.

What aint meet yuh don't pass yuh.
Just because you have not encountered somethind (usually bad) does not mean you'll never encounter it.

What do you get from a bag of coals? Dust.
A person is the product of his upbringing.

Yu livin like Miss Howard cat.
Used in reference to one who has no permanent abode.

FROM THE AFRICAN CONTINENT

A blind man may see with the eye of the soul .... Swahili

A coin in cash is better than ten on credit .... Bambara

A handful of luck is better than a
donkey load of learning .... North Africa

A man's love goes through his stomach.

A woman's love goes through her purse .... South Africa

A polite mouth opens doors .... South Africa

An old woman can outwit even the devil .... Morocco

Any mouth God opens he will put food in it .... Senegal

A tree cannot stand without its roots.

(A Government cannot exist without its people .... Zaire

Children are as dear to the heart
as they are to the pocket .... South Africa

Death is like a thief: He never announces his visit .... Congo

Do not make too many enemies all at once .... South Africa

Even if your mother is poor, she is still your mother .... Ovambo

Every heart knows its own suffering .... South Africa

76

Fools and infants do not lie .... Kunama

Friendship can neither be boughtsold .... Morroco

Give a beggar a finger, he will take the whole hand .... South Africa

Gossip is like a disease, once you have caught it,
it is hard to get rid of it.. Swahili

Home is where they bake the bread .... South Africa

If you are in one boat you have to row together .... South Africa

If you have no happiness at home,
you will not find it abroad .... Swahili

If your mother has not taught you, life will teach you .... Swahili

Kindness is the best remedy for suffering................... Mozambique

Knowledge is like an ocean: no man's arms can embrace it Swahili

Lending money is a sure way of buying an enemy ...... South Africa

Life is the best school – and the hardest .... South Africa

Love is like being possessed by
a spirit: lovers are not their own masters ....Zaire

Marriage – There is a lid for every pot,
and a key for every lock.. Swahili

Money cannot talk, yet it can make lies look truth..... South Africa

Money is the man. If you have none.
No one will love you .... Hausa

Money never makes the crooked straight.................... South Africa

One bad tongue can poison a village .... Kenya

Only a fool hates his family... Hausa

Sickness comes on a swift horse and
leaves on a slow donkey .... South Africa

Smoke cannot be hidden ....Burundi

Starting a war is easy. Ending it is not................................. Egypt

The best talent is a sharp ear and a good memory................. Kenya

The patient man eats ripe fruits .... Swahili

The tortoise carries his roof with him .... Swahili

Thoughts are free: no one can read them
or steal them .... South Africa

When two quarrel, two are guilty .... South Africa

FROM THE LANDS OF SOME OF OUR EARLIER SETTLERS

CHINA

A dog won't forsake his master because of his poverty; a son never deserts his mother for her homely appearance.

A smile will gain you ten more years of life.

A fall into a ditch makes you wiser.

An inch of time is an inch of gold but you can't buy that inch of time with an inch of gold.

Flies never visit an egg that has no crack.

Flowing water never goes bad: our door hubs never gather termites.

Have a mouth as sharp as a dagger, but a heart as soft as tofu.

If a son is uneducated, his dad is to blame.

If you do not study hard when young, you'll end up bewailing your failures as you grow up.

It is easy to dodge a spear that comes in front of you but hard to keep harms away from an arrow shot from behind.

One cannot refuse to eat just because there is a chance of being choked.

There are always ears on the other side of the wall.

Vicious as a tigeress can be, she never eats her own cub.

We are not so much concerned if you are slow as when you come to a halt.

When you are poor, neighbors close by will come; once you become rich, you'll be surprised by visits from (alleged) relataives afar.

With money you can buy a bed, but not sleep.

With money you can buy blood, but not life.

With money you can buy a book, but not knowledge.

With money you can buy a clock, but not time.

With money you can buy a doctor, but not health.

With money you can buy a house, but not a home.

With money you can buy a position, but not respect.

With money you can buy sex but not love.

Without rice, even the cleverest housewife cannot cook.

You can't catch a cub without going into the tiger's den.

ENGLAND

Action speaks louder than words.

Advice is least heeded when most needed.

A wise man changes his mind sometimes, a fool never.

All work and no play, makes Jack a dull boy.

An idle brain is the devil's workshop.

An ounce of prevention is worth a pound of cure.

Catch not at the shadow and loose the substance.

Children are what you make them.

Dead men tell no tales.

Discretion is the better part of valour.

Enough is as good as a feast.

Experience keeps a dear school, but fool will lean in no other.

Follow the river and you will find the sea.

Give a fool enough rope and he will hang himself.

If wishes were horses beggars would ride.

Look before you leap.

Lost time is never found.

Make hay while the sun shines.

Men are as old as they look. Women are as old as they feel.

Neither wise men nor fools can work without tools.

One man's meal is another man's poison.

Some men are wise and some are otherwise.

Strike the iron while it is hot.

There are more foolish buyers than foolish sellers.

What the eye does admire the heart does not admire.

HOLLAND

All things in their being are good for something.

A man's home is his castle.

A man is as old as he feels and a woman is as old as she looks.

Better be a poor man's darling than a rich man's fool.

Better keep than make peace.

Big words seldom go with big deeds.

Blood is thicker than water.

Boys will be boys.

Every Jack has his Jill.

He who would eat the fruit must climb the tree.

He who will not learn when he is young will regret it when he is old.

He who does not honor his wife, dishonors himself.

If you son don't know where you are going, any road will get you there.

It is never too late to learn.

It is better to give than to take.

Little is done where many command.

Love is blind.

One should eat to live, not live to eat.

Procastination is the thief of time.

While there is life there is hope.

The course of true love never runs smooth.

The important thing in life is to have a great aim, and the determination to attain it.

Two wrongs do not make a right.

You can't ride two horses at the same time.

We are here to add towhat we can to life, not to get what we can from it.

SPAIN

He who goes with wolves learns to howl.

He who looks for a mule without fault must go by foot.

How beautiful it is to do nothing, and then rest afterward.

If you can't bite don't show your teeth.

Jealousy knows no loyalty.

More things grow in the garden than the gardner sows.

The beginning of healh is to know the disease.

Where two will not, one cannot quarrel.

Who ventures nothing has no luck.

WALES

A fair exchange is no robbery.

A rolling stone gathers no moss.

A word to the wise is enough.

Brevity is the soul of wit.

Charity begins at home but should not end there.

Every man must carry his own cross.

Honest men marry soon, wise men not at all.

Kind words are worth much and cost little.

By others faults wise men correct their own.

Curses are like chickens, they come home to roost.

Do not count your chickens before they are hatached.

Every ass loves to hear himself bray.

Hasty climbers have sudden falls.

If you cannot make a man think as you do, make him do as you think.

Lend only what you can afford to loose.

Never trouble trouble until trouble troubles you.

Presents keep friendships warm.

Put not your trust in money; put your money in trust.

The devil lurks behind the cross.

The devil has three children. Pride, Falsehood, and Envy.

The world is a staircase; some are going up, some are coming down.

Those who live in glass houses should not throw stones.

We can live without our friends, but not without our neighbors.

When the wine is in, the wit is out.

Youth lives on hope, old age on remembrance.

Edna Bennett

FAVORITES
FROM
THE BIBLE

Proverbs in this section were originally written by King Solomon, hailed as the wisest man of his time. Solomon was a son of David, and was said to have written three thousand proverbs and many songs, known to Christians as the Songs of Solomon.

A felon will flee when no one is pursuing him.

A fool believes whatever he is told.

A fool cannot spend money wisely.

A fool will revert to his folly, just as a dog returns to his vomit.

A friend is a friend at all times.

A friend nearby is better than a brother far away.

A good name is better than riches.

A kind answer soothes anger; while a cutting word increases wrath.

A quiet tongue shows a wise head.
A simple meal offered with love is better than a feast offered without love.

A smile mirrors a happy heart.

Better to live in a deserted place than with a raging and abusive woman.

Boast not thyself of tomorrow; for thou knowest not what a day may bring.

Children's children are the crown of old men.

Contact with his neighbor can refine a man.

Fortune suddenly acquired will dwindle away, but fortune acquired a little at a time will bring about riches.

God made everything for its own purpose.

He who laughs at the deprived will not be unpunished.

He who mocks the poor insults their Creator.

Honor to a fool is as beneficial as snow is to summer.

Idleness is where the devil finds work.

If you befriend the wise, you can learn from him, but if you befriend a fool you will suffer for it.

Interfering in the quarrels of others is like catching a dog by the tail.

It is impossible to separate a fool from his folly.

It is unlikely for a fool to live in luxury, and less likely for a slave to rule princes.

Listen to advice; accept correction, to be the wiser in the time to come.

Man's heart seeks the right way, but it is Yahwey who makes his footsteps sure.

No man can serve two masters.

No one can share the joy or sorrow of another person's heart.

One will profit from hard work, but never from idle talk.

Ostentatious promises are like clouds and strong winds and no rain.

Sharp words provoke anger, but gentle words prevent anger.

Some friends are closer than a brother, others can lead you to ruin.

The borrower is the slave of the lender.

The idler turns on his bed just as a door turns on its hinges.

The price of wisdom is greater than the price of rubies.

To serenade a sorrowing heart is like pouring vinegar on an open wound.

Train a child in the way you want him to go, and even when he becomes an adult he will not leave it.

Where there are no talebearers there are fewer quarrels.

Where there is danger the wise avoids it, but the ignorant walks right into it.

PATOIS - A PROFILE

A Contribution

The Caribbean islands are very rich in their cultural expressions, commonly referred to as their 'accents'. These expressions are influenced by the early settlers on the island – the English, Spanish, Dutch and French.

Every island has its own way of pronouncing words which reflects its original settlers.

The Trinidadan ....fa so man....to mean, so it is.
The Barbadian .... flaig for flag, and baig for bag.
Of course you can't miss the Jamaican .... yes man, no man.

Gestures, laughter, shouting when in heated argument, are all a part of the spoken medium, and are often described as our Oral Culture. However, English is the official language of the Jamaican people, and our English grammar is in now way affected by our accent.

The early European settlers of the 16th and 17th centuries came from different parts of Europe, and they brought with them regional dialects. In addition they also came from different social strata, spoke different forms of English and different social dialects. The same can be said for the African slaves. They came from different regions of the African continent, were of different tribes and social strata, and spoke different African languages and dialects.

There was no formal education for slaves. The punishments were harsh when slaves failed to speak English. Slaves therefore, were forced to acquire the language of the ruling class in order to communicate with their masters. They also had to communicate with each other, hence the birth of the dialect form PATOIS.

Over the years, the generations that survived slavery were brainwashesd into believing that patois was socially unacceptable. We have come a long way since then.

In Jamaica, Use of English is a very strong component of Tutorial level education, and is on-going. Awareness and appreciation for the use of patois is being promoted at all levels of the education contimuum. In fact, so seriously that a patois dictionary is now being compiled, and hopefully will soon be published. There is no doubt that a lot of people are looking forward to this publication.

Jamaicans have matured. The wounds of slavery have healed, but the scars of slavery remain. We now view patois as yet another scar of slavery, one which the Jamaican people proudly bear.

GLOSSARY

(A)

Abeng: A shell blown by Maroons. These were runaway slaves who defied and defeated British soldiers by using guerilla tactics.

Abbey: Small hard-shelled fruit eaten by school-children.

Aerated water: Carbonated soft drink.

A fi mi: It is mine!

Alli-button: One who works for nothing.

Anansi: The leading man and hero in Jamaican folklore. Brer Anansi, who appears in   stories as a cunning spider, gets his name from the Ashanti word meaning spider.

Arnold: Name given to pork by those who have sworn not to eat pig products, but   secretly enjoy the taste. Also referred to as *Dat*, because the surreptitious buyer will point at the meat without calling its proper name.

Asham: Concoction made of ground corn and sugar.

(B)

Baboo: Nickname for a person with East Indian features.

Baby coffin: Shoes for very large feet.

Babylon: Used in reference to the police or an perceived agency of oppression.

Baby mother: An unwed female parent.

Baby father: Counterpart to the baby mother.

Backative: Backing, usually financial.

Back and front:	A snowball (shaved ice and syrup) with ice-cream topping.
Backiney:	Festivity to drive ghosts back into the grave.
Back answer:	A saucy response from a child to remarks made by his elders.
Backra:	A white person having wealth and great authority.
Backra better:	Mulatto who ingratiates himself with whites.
Bad bargain:	An unreliable person.
Bad no yaws:	Incorrigibly bad.
Balm-yard:	The operational headquarters of obeahmen and others dealing in the supernatural.
Bamboo root:	A fibrous ball made from the root of the bamboo tree and used by small boys playing cricket.
Bam-bye:	Future date (by and by).
Bammy:	A small, round cake made from the grated root of the cassava plant.
Bandana cloth:	Colorful material of red and blue made in India and used in making a national costume. Also used to make a *cotta*.
Bandoolu:	Illegal.
Bangarang:	Commotion.
Bang belly:	Extended abdomen caused by malnutrition.
Bankra:	A basket.
Bannabis:	A bea mush used by the poor.
Barbecue:	Concrete platform used for drying spices.
Bat and ball:	Game of cricket.
Batty:	The posterior.
Batty and Bench:	A term used to describe two persons who are always close together.
Batty outta door:	Pants torn at the seat, exposing the posterior.
Beat-it:	The term used to describe the act of getting into an event surreptitiously and without paying the required fee.
Beat-out:	Exhausted.
Bed-jay:	Makeshift bed.

Beeps: Homosexual.

Belly come down: Hernia. Said to be the effects of distress.

Belly-lick: Dance in which the partners bounce off each other's abdomen.

Belly woman: Woman in the state of pregnancy.

Ben' down: Goods sold from under the counter.

Ben Johnson Day: Any day when food and money are scarce.

Best butter: Used to differentiate fresh butter from *salt butter*.

Bickle: Food.

Big brains: Smart aleck.

Big foot: A disease that is inflicted on victims by an obeahman, sometimes called *big- foot man*.

Bigga: A man with a tall, thick-set physique.

Big tree man: One of a group of bullies who were stationed beneath the banyan trees in the old Victoria Park, Kingston.

Bissy: Cola nut.

Bit: Four and a half pennies.

Bitch-up: Roughly constructed.

Black-up: A state of drunkenness. Also used in describing the darkenening sky that precedes rainfall.

Bleach: To stay out late at night.

Bleaching stone: Stone on which washing is put in the sun to bleach.

Blouse and skirt: Expression of surprise.

Board horse: A small sliver of wood used by boys who race than in running water.

Boderation: Trouble.

Booby egg: The small, speckled egg of the sooty tern. It is eaten hard-boiled and sprinkled with salt and pepper.

Boogooyagga: A person of inferior social status.

Boonoonoonos: A person or thing regarded as very beautiful.

Boops: Sugar daddy. A man who keeps supporting an unfaithful woman.

Bottle lamp: A device made from a bottle containing kerosene and stuffed with paper or cloth, which serves as a wick.

Box and board: Makeshift bed consisting of slats laid on two boxes.

Brawta: Extra amount, also, *mek-up*.

Bredda: Brother.

Breeze-blow: Windstorm.

Breshey: Breadfruit.

Bringle: Irate.

Brought-upsy: Good home training.

Bruckins: Festivities.

Bruck yu ducks: Make a start; do something for the first time.

Bruise blood: Contusion.

Buck and kick: A water tank constructed of lime mortar.

Buggas: Boot made from canvas and rubber; sneakers.

Bulla: A small cake, round and flat. It is made with flour, dark brown sugar, and baking soda. A crispier version, made with light brown sugar, is called *mess-around*.

Bull bucker: The full term, *Bull bucker and duppy conqueror*, is used in reference to a pugnacious person who can defeat all comers, whether human, animal, or supernatural.

Bully beef: Canned corned beef.

Bully-rige: Overawe.

Bungo: Idiot.

Bu'n pan: A rectangular cooking pan used on a wood fire and deeply stained with soot. This type of vessel is also known as a *kerosene pan* as it is commonly used to store kerosene oil, following its original use as a cooking oil container.

Bun bad lamp: Work witchcraft; create mischief to embarrass another.

Buru: Rattling drum.

Burying ground: Cemetery.

Busha:	Overseer on a farm.
Bush tea:	Hot beverage made from herbs or leaves picked from the countryside.
Busta backbone:	A tough candy made of sugar and coconut.
Butter bun:	The insult and humiliation that a man is said to sustain when his mate is sexually unfaithful.
Bwoy:	Boy.

(C)

Cajones:	Having courage.
Callaband:	Trap for catching ground birds.
Cammarung:	Disreputable hanger-on. A bird that never builds its own nest.
Candy bump:	Hairstyle in which the hair is rolled into bumps instead of being plaited.
Candy leg:	Skinny leg.
Capoose:	Capers.
Carry-down:	To rob or betray. One who does this frequently is called a *carry-down artist*.
Carrying straw:	Courting, like birds building a nest.
Cask-water:	Very intoxicating drink made from water left to rest in a rum cask emptied of its alcoholic contents.
Cass-cass:	Quarrel; dispute.
Catta tick:	Drum stick.
Cauchie:	Loud whistle used by factories to indicate time to begin or end work.
Cietful:	Used to describe one who carries tales and cannot be trusted with a secret.
Chaka-chaka:	Untidy; in dissaray.
Charles Pryce:	Large cane-piece rat.
Chew-stick:	Stick chewed and used as a brush to clean the teeth.
Chi-chi:	Termite that attacks wooden furniture.

Chigger-foot:	One whose toes are attacked by the chigger mite. A sign of depravity involving the lack of shoes and frquenting of insanitary places.
Chiney shop:	Grocery store operated by Chinese retailers. The saying was derived from the fact that at one time the running of grocery shops was the exclusive business of Chinese immigrants.
Clammy cherry:	Small white berry eaten by schoolchildren.
Coarse salt:	Rock salt; used to differentiate between *fine salt*, which is used in cooking.
Cockaty:	Concieted.
Cock yu ears:	To listencarefully, surreptitously.
Cocobey:	A skin rash that is believed to result from frog spit, which is also known as *cuckoo spit.*
Coconut bat:	A cricket bat fashioned from the broad part of a dried coconut bough.
Coconut water:	Liquid contents of the green cocnut; used as a refreshing drink.
Coconut milk:	Juice extracted from the flesh of the dried coconut.
Coir mattress:	Bedding that has been stuffed with fiber taken from the husk of the coconut.
Come-see come-saw:	Neither good nor bad.
Condense pan:	Tin can used for holding condensed milk.
Coney Island:	Amusement park with a variety of attractions, including rides, games and music. The name was copied from New York's Coney Island; in Jamaica it became generic.
Cool drink:	Homemade ginger beer.
Coolie-foot:	a semi-white sugar.
Coolie man:	Nickname for one of Indian descent, derived from the days when large numbers of East Indians worked as coolies on agricultural estates.

Coolie plum:	Small greenish fruit with a single rough seed.
Copastetic:	All right.
Cork and tar:	Cricket ball made of cork and glue.
Cork yu ears:	Don't listen.
Coroaches:	Rubbish; useless items.
Corned:	State of drunkenness. Also referred to as *black-up*.
Cotch:	Object used to prevent movement, i.e. door, car. Also means temporary lodging or the act of resting.
Cotta:	Ring-shaped cushion placed on the head when carrying baskets.
Cow cod:	Penis of the bull; used to make a soup reputed to be an aphrodisiac.
Cow itch:	Plant or pod covered with fine particles that cause severe itching when it comes in contact with the skin. Cows feeding in the bushes are often affected by it.
Crab toe:	Illegible scribbling.
Crepe:	Canvas shoe made of rubber soles; a tennis shoe.
Criss:	Fresh and crisp; presenting a nice appearance.
Crocus bag:	Sack made from jute and used by farmers to carry just about everything requiring a bag.
Crosses:	Hardships.
Crow bait:	Used to describe one in very bad shape, dirty and dying. Also sneeringly associated with *probate*.
Crumugin:	Miserly, curmudgeon.
Cubba:	African name given to a boy born on Tuesday. *Miss Cubba* refers to an effeminate man.
Cubbitch:	Covetous, mean and stingy. A depression at the back of the neck is described as the *cubbitch hole*, and its depth is supposed to indicate the degree of a person's meanness.

Cubby hole:	Small, secret cache.
Cunny:	Clever; resourceful.
Cucatoo:	Basket used to press juice from the cassava when making bammies.
Cut eye:	A movement of the eye to show disgust.
Cut ten:	Posture is which one leg is crossed over the other while sitting.
Cut cake:	Confectionery made from coconut-boiled brown sugar.

(D)

Dark eye:	Poor eyesight.
Dawg:	Dog.
Dawg cornpiece:	A difficult situation. One is in deep trouble when caught in *dawg cornpiece*.
Dawg newspaper:	Rumor-mongering.
Dead house:	Morgue.
Deputy:	Married man's girlfriend.
Dibi dibi:	Inconsequential.
Dickance:	Extraordinary. One has dickance of a time at a party. On the other hand, he may be given the dickance by a tormentor.
Digging song:	Refrain vocalized by field workers. The lead singer, called a *raiser* sets the tone with a short phrase called *boblin*.
Dildo:	A tall member of the cactus family, usually grown as a fence around the homes of the poor.
Dilly:	Duckling.
Dinki mini:	Dancing and rites performed in connection with the death of a person.
Dip and fall back:	A stew made of salt mackerel cooked with coconut milk. Also known as *rundown*.
Diss:	To show disespect.
Dog romping:	Noisy game of catch and tag.

Done grow:	Adolescent who is small for his age.
Don'keah:	Careless.
Doo!:	Please!
Doo doo:	Faeces.
Doubloon:	Ancient Spanish coin.
Doubloon a joint:	Considered to be highly expensive.
Drape-up:	To have one's trousers pulled up by the waist, usually by a policeman.
Dreadlocks:	Rastafarian hair-style, in which the hair is grown long and matted.
Drop pan:	Numbers game played by gamblers.
Dry eye:	Bare-faced.
Dry foot:	Very slender legs.
Dry head:	Short, kinky hair.
Dry-land tourist:	Native who behaves like a tourist.
Duck ants:	Termites.
Duck bread:	Ceremonial loaf shaped like a duck, sometimes with ducklings.
Duckunoo:	A cornmeal pone cooked in a wrapping made from the leaf of the banana. Other names for this are *tie-leaf* and *blue drawers*.
Ducta:	Bus conductor.
Dundoos:	Albino.
Dungle:	Dunghill.
Duppy:	Ghost; a haunting spirit.
Duppy cherry:	Very small fruit said to be enjoyed by *duppies*.
Duppy umbrella:	Fungi resembling mushrooms.
Dutch pot:	Iron pot, sometimes made with three legs.
Dutty:	Dirty; ground.

(E-F)

Eye water:	Tears.
Face man:	Handsome male.
Facety:	Fiesty; saucy.
Fas' (fast):	Inquisitive.

Favour:	Resemble.
Fenke fenke:	Half-hearted.
Festival:	Fried roll made with flour, cornmeal and sugar.
Fever grass:	Lemon grass.
Finger smith:	Thief; pickpocket.
Fippance:	Three-penny piece.
Fire-stick:	Stick with a glowing ember at one end.
Fish head:	Bribe.
Fish tea:	Fish broth.
Flaw flaw:	Saltfish fritters.
Fling stone behind you:	To leave with no intention of returning.
Foo-foo:	Mixture of mashed yam, coco, plaintain and sweet potato.
Fool fool:	Mentally retarded.
Foot bottom:	Sole of the foot.
Force ripe:	A juvenile acting as an adult.
Forty legs:	A small, harmless millipede.
'Fraidy fraidy:	Timid.
Free paper:	Freedom; derived from the written statement given to indentured workers after their period of service on the plantations.
French letter:	A condom.
Fresco:	Semi-frozen mixture of milk and syrup.
Fretration:	Worry.
Fry fish shop:	Description of a disorganized business.
Fun and joke aside:	No fooling!
Fundeh:	Drum used in folk music

(G)

Galang:	Go quickly.
Ganja:	Marijuana; also called *sensimillia*.
Garden boy:	One in a subservient position.
Garden egg:	Fruit of the egg plant.
Gaulin:	A white-feathered heron.

Gawd blimey:	Boot made of canvas with rubber soles.
Geow:	An attempt to hoodwink.
Gill:	Three farthings.
Ginger:	Sore toe.
Gypsy:	A way of using English words to obscure their meaning.
Give an eye:	To monitor a situation.
Gizada:	Small, hard-shelled pie crust filled with a mixture of sugar and grated coconut.
Goat mouth:	Description given to one who's forecast of trouble is often correct.
Gone clear:	Out of danger and on the way to success.
Boombay:	Drum used in folk music.
Gourdy:	Calabash.
Grand market:	Christmas Eve sale.
Grater cake:	Sweet made from grated coconut and sugar.
Gravalicious:	Greedy.
'Gree:	Agree.
Green bush:	Used in treating insect bites; three different green leaves are rubbed together and applied to the affected part.
Ground dove:	Small brown bird that spends most of its time on the ground.
Ground provisions:	Edible roots, such as yams, potatoes, etc.
Grudgeful:	Envious.
Guard:	Objects worn by clients of sorcerers to protect themselves from evil spirits.
Guineagogg:	Champion.
Gully bean:	Susumber; a small, bitter berry eaten with saltfish.
Guzum:	Voodoo; black magic.

(H)

Haffoo:	Yam.
Hog sty:	Swelling of the eyelid; said to affect one who repossesses a gift.

Hang fire:	Wait.
Happy riddance:	A welcome departure or termination.
Hard dough:	Firm type of flour bread.
Hard ears:	Stubborn; impervious to advice.
Hard-pay man:	One who has to be dunned to pay his debts.
Hard socks:	Soft shoes.
Heavy manners:	Stern discipline.
Heng-pon-nail:	Ill-fitting clothes.
Higgler shop:	Shack in which assorted goods are sold.
Hill and gully riding:	A song game.
Hol' a fresh:	Take a bath.
Hot hops:	Unchilled beer.
Howdy:	How do you do, a greeting.
Hurry come up:	Upstart.
Hurro hurro:	Bits and pieces of cheap meat.
Hussay (Hassein):	Annual festival celebrated by Jamaicans of East Indian heritage.

(I)

I an' I:	Me alone.
Irie:	Irate; also used to describe something satisfying.
Ironie:	Ball-bearing used as a marble.
Ital:	Food prepared without salt.

(J)

Jackass corn:	A hard, sweet biscuit.
Jackass rope:	Tobacco leaves rolled into the form of a rope.
Jacket:	Child born to a woman who has been unfaithful to her recognized mate.
Jack Mandora:	Mythological character referred to in a disclaimer at the end of Anansi stories "Jack Mandora, mi no choose none."
Jail bud:	One who spends a lot of time in jail.

Janga:	Type of shrimp found in rivers.
Jeng jeng:	Riff-raff.
Jerk:	Style of cooking meat over an open fire with plenty of spices. First used by Maroons.
Jestering:	Making threats without having any intention of carrying them out.
Jew water:	Dewdrops.
Jimmy-swing:	Commonplace.
Jinnal:	Swindler.
Jippi jappa:	A straw hat.
John Canoe:	Traditional street dancer, wearing costume of rags, small mirrors, animal heads, etc.
John Crow:	Turkey vulture that feeds on carrion.
John Crow batty:	Crude, strong rum.
John Crow bead:	Brightly colored seed used by peasants in making necklaces.
Johnny cake:	Small, round quick bread that is fried instead of baked. Also called a *journey cake*.
Johnny Cooper:	Musical beat made by one cleaning a floor with a cocunut brush.
Jokify:	Jovial.
Jook:	Prick or penetrate.
Joota:	Heavy leather boot.
Junjo:	Mushroom or fungus.

(K)

K-Foot:	Knock-kneed.
Keepup:	A game in which a small object is kept airborne by short kicks.
Kerosene pan:	Oblong container made of zinc and used for storing oil, boiling clothes, cooking food or carrying water.
Ketch:	Catch.
Ketch yu 'fraid:	Become alarmed.
Key-soap time:	Difficult time, derived from an advertisement for a brand of soap claiming to be very hard.

Kibber:	Close; shut.
Kick-the-bucket:	To die.
Kirrout!:	Get away!
Kiss teeth:	Gesture of insolence or defiance.
Kiss mi neck:	Expression of surprise.
Kitchen bitch:	Tin lamp using kerosene.
Koo dey!:	Look there!
Koo yah!:	Look here!
Kreng kreng:	A type of basket.
Ku ku macca:	A heavy stick used in fighting intruders and attackers.
Kumina:	Folk dance celebrating love, birth, growth and departure from life.
Kunnu munnu:	Stupid person; one easily manipulated.

(L)

Labrish:	Gossip.
Lamps:	To hoodwink, lampoon.
Langu lawla:	Tall, skinny person.
Las' lick:	Game played by children; the final act.
Lawta:	A wide flat pan used for cooking.
Lay table:	To direct an evil spirit against one's adversaries.
Leggins:	Bundle of vegetables used in making soup; legumes.
Level:	Levy.
Lickle:	Small.
Licky licky:	Greedy.
Liges:	Favoritism.
Lilly:	Small.
Lines:	Ways and means other than the traditional.
Line stick:	A long stick used to brace a burdened clothesline.
Love bush:	Parasitic vine usually found on hedges.
Low bite:	One very low on the social scale.

(M)

Maama man:	Effeminate male.
Macca:	Thorn.
Macca fat:	Small shelled fruit eaten by children.
Madda young gal:	Older woman who dresses or behaves like a young girl.
Maggidge:	Blemish caused by the fruit fly.
Mampala:	Man who likes to do woman's work.
Man-boy:	Boy acting like a grown-up; also *Man-too.*
Mannish water:	Soup made from the head and fifth quarter of goats; also called *suluwa.*
Maroon:	Runaway slave.
Mash mout':	When the front teeth are missing.
Mawga:	Meager; thin.
Merriwang:	Stringed instrument made from calabash, cowhide and a cedar handle.
Mess-aroun':	Small round cake resembling a bulla.
Missis Queen:	Queen Victoria.
Monkey fiddle:	A type of cactus, the branches of which can be rubbed together to make a sound.
Monkey jar:	Clay jar used for storing water.
Moonshine baby:	Game played by moonlight in which the outline of a person is made with broken glass or crockery.
Moreish:	Something nice, requiring a second helping.
Morning sport:	Exchange of labor in which the participants collaborate in helping to plough land or build houses. Each host in turn provides food and drink.
Mout':	Sass; to upbraid.
Mout'-a-massy:	Chatterbox.
Mouth-water cloth:	Necktie.
Mumma:	Mother.

(N)

Naana:	Unlicensed midwife.
Nankeen:	Type of cotton cloth.
Natty dread:	Rastafarian.
Natty head:	Hair that is kinky and difficult to comb.
Nayga:	Negro.
Needle case:	Dragonfly.
Niggeritis:	Tendency to sleep after eating.
Night glass:	Chamber pot; also called *chimmy*.
Night owl:	One who is very active on the streets at night.
Nine-night:	Wake, marking the ninth night after an individual's death.
Nuff:	Plenty.
Nyanga:	Pride.
Nyam:	To eat heartily.

(O)

Obeah:	Sorcery.
Old Hige:	Name given to a pest.
Old Man beard:	Moss that grows on utility wires.
Oonu:	You all.
Ooman:	Woman.

(P)

Packy:	Calabash.
Pan head:	District constable.
Partner:	System of cooperative saving in which participants take turns in drawing the pot every week or month.
Pasero:	Close friend.
Pay fi roas' an' bwile:	To be served the fullest punishment.

Peaka Peaw:	Petty; unimportant.
Peel neck:	Domestic fowl with a neck devoid of feathers.
Peeny wally:	Small bug that displays a light when it flies at night.
Pepperpot:	Soup made from a mix of greens boiled with pickled pig's tail and salt-beef.
Pinchey cobie:	Stingy person.
Pick a bone:	Argue a point.
Pickney:	Child.
Pinda:	Peanut.
Ping wing:	A prickly plant of the pineapple family. A distortion of the word *penguin*.
Patoo:	Owl.
Plate cloth:	Rag used to wash dishes.
Play three:	To die. In *drop pan*, the number three is associated with death.
Pocomania:	Religious rite in which the worshipers engage in frenzied dancing before going into a trance.
Poorist:	Tourist without much money.
Poor thing:	One forsaken and impecunious.
Pop sport:	To have a real good time.
Pop story:	Invitation to gossip.
Poppy show:	Puppet show; one who is the subject of mockery.
Pricky pear:	Fruit of the cactus.
Pupil teacher:	Student teacher.
Puppalick:	Somerault.
Putus:	A nice girl.
Puss boots:	Canvas shoe with rubber sole.

(Q)

Q-Q:	Quart-quart; term used to describe a half-pint rum flask or its contents.
Quaco:	Character from Anansi stories.

Quashie:	Very ordinary person, having no influence and attracting little respect. Also, African name given to boys born on Sunday.
Quattie:	Penny and a half.

(R)

Rahtid:	Expression of surprise, also used adjectively to describe the superlative.
Rake:	Intuition.
Ram goat roses:	Periwinkle.
Rastafarian:	Member of a religion worshiping the late Ethiopian emporer, Haile Sellasie. Before becoming emporer, his title was Ras Tafari.
Rat cut:	Used to describe coffee or cocoa beans nibbled by rats.
Rat passage:	Stowaway.
Ratta:	Rat.
Red eye:	Covetous.
Red Ibo:	Negro of very light complexion.
Red seam:	Regular policeman whose uniform includes a broad red band running down the outer side of each leg of the trousers.
Rhynin:	Superlatively good or bad.
Riddle:	Game in which folk phrases are used in proposing a puzzle for the audience to solve.
Ring ding:	Ruckus.
Roadster:	A last drink before hitting the road.
Roast:	Job undertaken by a worker outside of his normal employment.
Roast breadfruit:	Description of a black person with white affectations.
Rolling calf:	Mythical animal that wanders about at night; also a restless person.
Rowasome:	Quarrelsome.

Rub-up:	Dance in which the partners hold each other closely.
Rungus:	Artifice.
Runnings:	Happenings.
Rush and score:	Soccer game in which players change positions at will.

(S)

Salt:	Having persistent bad luck.
Salt t'ings:	Any salted or pickled fish or meat.
Samfie:	Cunning rascal.
Sam patta:	A homemade slipper.
Sankey:	Religious chorus, originally written by English songwriter, Ira D. Sankey.
Say fey!:	I dare you!
Scandal bag:	Plastic bag that makes a crackling sound when it is being handled.
Science-man:	One dealing in witchcraft.
Screw-face:	Wearing a frown.
Scrub dry yaws:	To ingratiate oneself.
Scruffler:	One who makes a living by odd jobs and devious endeavours.
Seen?:	Understood.
Sensay:	A type of fowl with curled feather.
Set girls:	Group of dancers who were a feature of social events in the period following slavery.
Set up:	A wake held by relatives to mourn the dead.
Sheg up:	Spoilt; work done badly.
Shoe-black:	The hibiscus flower, sometimes used to clean shoes.
Show bread:	Bread used as a display at fundraising tea parties. At the end of the festivities, it is shared by all the participants.
Shut:	Shirt.

Shut bag:	Bag carried over the shoulder by farmers.
Shut pan:	Pan with a tight-fitting lid, used for carrying food, etc.
Siddung:	Sit down.
Sinkle bible:	Aloe vera.
Sinting:	Something.
Sipple:	Slippery.
Skin teeth:	To grin.
Skull:	To skip school or an assignment.
Sky juice:	Rain; also used to describe a mixture of shaved ice, syrup and water.
Smaddy:	Somebody.
Snowball:	Shaved ice, flavored with fruit syrup.
Soak up:	Spoilt.
Soldering:	Love-making.
Soldier Peggy:	Prostitute who favors the company of soldiers.
So so:	Only.
Sour sop heart:	Eaten as a cure for bed wetting.
Spliff:	Marijuana cigarette.
Spree bwoy:	Fun-loving male.
Spring chicken:	Frog.
Stale drunk:	Hangover.
Stamp an' go:	Fritter made from flour and saltfish.
Steel bottom:	Mixture of rum and beer.
Stocious:	Pleasing to the eye.
Stocking head:	Top of a woman's pantyhose, cut off and tied to form a headgear; often worn to keep a man's hair in place.
Stone dawg:	Used to describe a situation in which a product is in oversupply: *"Mi have mango fi stone dawg."*
Stray shot:	Illegitimate child.
Stroke catcher:	Male sexual libertine.
Strong back:	A root used in the making of folk tonics.
Supple jack:	Leather thong used as a whip.

Su su:	Gossip.
Sweet mout':	Flatter or flattery.
Sufferer:	One experiencing hardship and deprivation.
Sugar head:	Product make of hardened sugar.

(T)

Tacooma:	Anansi's brother.
Tallawah:	Strong and vigorous. A person may be described as being *little but tallawah.*
Tan tuddy:	Keep quiet!
Tamarind season:	Time of scarcity.
Tam'rind switch:	Whip made of three sticks from the tamarind tree. Once used to flog prisoners for certain offenses.
Tea meeting:	Social gathering at which singers and dancers perform and the audience pays them off the stage or continue with their act. The "chairman" presides with high-sounding phrases and big words. Participants also pay to see a "queen" or *show-bread* unveiled.
Tie teeth:	Chewy confectionery made from sugar and grated coconut.
Tiki tiki:	A small fish.
Till dawg 'fraid:	Until very late at night.
Ting-a-merry:	Something unidentified.
Tinkng toe:	A hard-shelled fruit with seeds and covered with a powderey substance that is eaten by school lchildren.
Toe a beg bread:	When the toe is exposed through a hole in the socks or shoes.
Toona:	A member of the cactus family, used for washing hair.
Top rankin':	Highly rated.
Try it nuh:	An invitation or dare.
Tumpa-foot:	Peg-leg.

Edna Bennett

Tu'n duck offa nes':	To remove a person from a long-held position.
Tu'n fool:	To be stunned.
Tupse:	Small amount.
Turn stick:	Stick with a broad end, used to stir large pots of food.

(U-V-W)

Under the clock:	To be born under the clock is to be born in Kingston, the capital city.
Village lawyer:	Uneducated person who assumes the role of adviser on a multiplicity of subjects.
Wagga wagga:	Plentiful. _Version: Like dirt._
Walker and Kickstone:	The mythical company for which the unemployed are said to work.
Walk good:	Have a pleasant journey.
Warra warra:	A person's private parts or business.
Wash:	Mixture of water and dark-brown sugar, sometimes with the addition of lime juice.
Wash belly:	A woman's last child.
Wash-out:	Action of a laxative.
Wass wass:	Wasp.
Water coconut:	Liquid from a green coconut.
Water knee:	Painful knee that sometimes affects soccer players.
Water mouth:	Dribbling.
Waters:	Rum and other alcoholic spirits.
Whats-it-not:	Sundry parts of the body.
Whites:	Overproof white rum.
Winjie:	Wizened.

Wishy washy:	Substandard.
Wiss wiss:	Vine produced by a tropical tree.
Woman tongue:	Tree bearing a long, broad pod, which makes noises when the wind blows.
Worldian:	Man of the world, used by churchgoers to describe those who love secular pursuits.
Would-like-to-be:	A social aspirant.

(Y-Z)

Yard:	Home.
Yard-boy:	Young male employed to do odd jobs around the home.
Yabba:	Clay pot used for cooking.
Yearry:	Hear.
Yu post me:	You kept me waiting in vain!
Youthman:	Male adolescent.
Zinc pan:	Sixteen-quart container used for a variety of purposes.

ABOUT THE AUTHOR

EDNA BENNETT is the seventh of nine children born to Wilmot and Madeline Williams of Jamaica, West Indies. She was born in Kingston, the island's capital, got her early education there and became a trained nurse. She received her general nursing training at the Kingston School of Nursing, her midwifery training at the Victoria Jubilee Lying-In Hospital and her public health training at the West Indies School of Public Health. Over the years 1956-63, she worked as an RN in Canada and returned to Jamaica for further study of her profession as well as of her cultural roots. In 1972, Mrs. Bennett was trained as a Family Planning Clinician and worked as a Parish Clinic Nurse for the five years that followed. She considers her work in family planning and family-planning and family-life education as the highlight of her career.

In 1985, Mrs. Bennett graduated from the University of the West Indies as a nursing administrator and worked in this capacity until 1987, when she and her family immigrated to the United States. She is married to Vincent A. Bennett, Jr. They have a daughter, Alison and a son, Walter. She is now a widow, and the proud grand mother of four grand-children; Ibrahim, Nickayla, Fatima and Nikyle.

ABOUT THE EDITOR

KEN JONES has given distinguished service in many fields, including journalism, public relations and community service, both in Jamaica and the United States. In 1987, his work was publicly recognized by his appointment as a commander of the Order of Distinction.

He has edited several publications, worked in radio and television, and was executive director of the Jamaica Information Service, 1980-84.

His most recent professional post was as community relations coordinator, based in the New York Consulate General, working among Jamaicans living in the United States and Canada. Mr. Jones has now retired, and has returned to Jamaica.

TRIBUTES

It has been a Bible for me and will serve as a cultural dictionary far beyond Jamaica.
The future will always remember that you documented the past and did so without losing your own identity ......Alex Pascal,
Lecturer, London, UK

My heartiest congratulations go to Edna Bennett for the collecting and collating Popular Jamaican Sayings. My wish is that the collection will be made available to schools, tiertery institutions, and all those persons interested in the sociology of the Jamaican people. Correctly interpreted, these sayings could help considerably in understanding the wisdom of the Jamaican and his attitude to life..Hon. Sir Howard F. Cooke,
Governor - general of
Jamaica

"For all the true lovers
of folklore..................................... Professor C. C. Ifemesia,
Director,
Center for African American Studies,
Adelphi University, Long Island,
New York